APL
A Design Handbook for Commercial Systems

WILEY SERIES IN INFORMATION PROCESSING

Consulting Editor
Mrs Steve Shirley OBE, *F. International Limited, UK*

Visual Display Terminals
A. Cakir, D. J. Hart, and T. F. M. Stewart

Managing Systems Development
J. S. Keen

Face to File Communication
Bruce Christie

APL – A Design Handbook for Commercial Systems
Adrian Smith

APL
A Design Handbook
for Commercial Systems

Adrian Smith
Rowntree Mackintosh, York, England

1807 1982

JOHN WILEY & SONS

Chichester · New York · Brisbane · Toronto · Singapore

005.133
A 6425

British Library Cataloguing in Publication Data:
Smith, Adrian
 APL: a design handbook for commercial systems.
 −(Wiley series in information processing)
 1. APL (computer program language)
I. Title
001.64'24   QA76.73.A27

ISBN 0 471 10092 7

Library of Congress Cataloging in Publication Data:
Smith, Adrian, 1953−
 APL, a design handbook for commercial systems.
 −(Wiley series in information processing)
 Includes index.
 1. APL (Computer program language) 2. Business
−Data processing.   I. Title   II. Series.
HF5548.5.A23S62   001.64'24   81−16010

ISBN 0 471 10092 7   AACR2

Typeset by Activity, Salisbury, Wilts
and printed by The Pitman Press, Bath, Avon

Contents

Preface and acknowledgements

Two character traits must be held responsible for this book: my inability to pass by any interesting tit-bit of programming wisdom without picking it up and filing it; and my plain straightforward laziness. The trouble about being the curator of a pile of useful odds 'n' ends is that people keeping pestering you about it – what better way to fob them off than to put all the juiciest morsels in a book and then persuade them to buy it? With a bit of luck one or two others might buy it too, a side-effect to which I could hardly object!

Of course *really* lazy people rarely get around to the actual writing bit – for the fact that this one did finally make it into manuscript you must blame my wife. Her knack of sitting down meaningfully behind the typewriter and glaring at me provided just sufficient stimulus to keep me going. She also deserves my thanks for draughting the figures, sorting out the more disastrous bits of punctuation, and ruthlessly exposing waffle.

My colleagues in operational research and systems development have been both source and proving ground for the bulk of the material – I am obviously immensely grateful to them for their help and tolerance; in particular I would like to thank Harry Clough for his critical review of Chapter 12. The UK APL user group has contributed a lot of code and ideas, as have the newsletters of I. P. Sharp and APL*PLUS (STSC Inc) – I am greatly indebted to all of them.

Finally, I must thank the staff of my company's word-processing centre for accepting without murmur a long succession of redrafts, and IBM for printing the APL code in camera-ready form.

Introduction:
APL's place in commercial computing

This book is about the use of APL in commercial computing. It does not pretend to be a definitive text; rather an exploration of possibilities; an attempt to put together in a reasonably logical order my experiences of writing a totally new breed of commercial system.

I suspect that APL may come to be classed as one of the happiest accidents ever to befall computing. On the face of it, the APL notation has virtually nothing to recommend it to the commercial user: it is the antithesis of everything he expects from a programming language! It is terse in the extreme, needs specially adapted keyboards and printers, and is interpreted rather than compiled. Now everyone knows that commercial systems must be easy to maintain and efficient to run; what on Earth can the business user want with a funny Greek language that is interpreted backwards?!

What I hope to show in this volume is that there is an enormous tract of territory which has been left largely unexplored and under-exploited by the traditional computing methods. In general I am talking about systems for planning, decision support, and management information -- systems where change comes unexpectedly and often, and where the need to react quickly is paramount. I am convinced that APL is by far the best tool yet invented for building such systems, and I hope that in my first few chapters I can pass some of this conviction on to you. However, I am also sure that APL, like all powerful tools, is capable of doing a great deal of damage if mishandled; equally much of its potential may never be realized if it is used excessively cautiously!

In the central part of the book I want to develop a philosophy - and eventually a methodology - for system design with APL. This I hope will show you where you can best use APL, and how you should set about building an APL system. The material in Chapters 8-11 covers in detail the APL functions and idioms which I have found most helpful in design, maintenance, and documentation. I have also gone to some lengths to include a number of timed examples, which I hope will demonstrate that a well written APL system can often provide a more efficient answer than a similar system in a compiled language.

Perhaps I should make it clear that this is not a textbook of APL - if you want to find out in detail what all these funny symbols do, then the Appendix reviews a selection of the available literature. However, I think that a couple of chapters (4 and 8) could well be of interest to an APL novice, as examples of the way an APL program looks in practice. The same applies to parts of Chapter 10, where I have used some screen-design functions as an extended example of the way an APL application should be structured.

1

To say that interactive computing is moving fast would be the understatement of the decade! I have no idea where we shall be in 10 years' time, but I'm sure that many of the systems being written today will still be about - maybe much modified - then. Accordingly I am going to devote my final chapter to a decidely speculative look ahead, in the hope that what we build today can at least form a firm foundation for the systems of the future.

Chapter 1

A break with the past

'That funny Greek language that executes backwards'
Anon.

APL is not a computer language. It is a general purpose mathematical notation, developed independently of computers, which has been slightly adapted so that its expressions can be evaluated by computers in a tailor-made environment. This distinction is fundamental; it makes a nonsense of any attempt at point-for-point comparisons of APL with the FORTRANs and COBOLs of this world, and it explains much of the culture shock felt by anyone trained in a conventional language when he or she is first faced with APL. In this chapter I hope to achieve two things: first, to emphasize the gulf between APL and conventional computer languages; secondly, to show that the time-honoured methods of systems analysis were a consequence of these languages, and that APL makes much of the conventional wisdom obsolete.

I think the best way to start is with a bit of history, so I would like to begin with a very brief review of how (and why) computer languages came about. In the early days, the only way to instruct a computer was to enter the binary codes (which drove the electronics) directly into its memory. It is still theoretically possible to do this, and in fact it is coming back into fashion with home computers, as hobbyists rediscover the early days of the art. The biggest problem with 'machine-code' programming is the difficulty of grasping what all these codes do. The human brain can cope with logical concepts like 'Add the contents of the memory at location 457 to the Accumulator' quite well, but '10000110'?! So were born the first ASSEMBLERS, the first real attempt to communicate with computers on our terms.

What an assembly language does is to automate the conversion of logical concepts into the binary signals needed to instruct the electronics. It also lets you give names to areas in the memory, so that you could write the instruction above as something like 'ADD A, SALES', assuming, of course, you tell the computer that SALES is at memory position 457! To write a computer program (i.e. a logically arranged series of instructions) in an assembly language is obviously a far less daunting task than writing it in machine code. What is more, once the program has been assembled it will make very efficient use of the computer; which is why assembly language is still used wherever the efficiency of the resulting program outweighs everything else.

Assemblers, however, are only the start of the story. Since even quite clever computers can recognize only a hundred or so different instructions, an assembler's repertoire is terribly limited. Before real-life problems can be tackled they must first be expressed as a sequence of these instructions; this is often difficult and always time-consuming. To see what I mean, take an (ostensibly) simple problem and see just what a sort of meal the assembler language makes of it.

'Add up SALES, and call the result TOTAL'

Using the assembler for the popular Z-80 micro-computer, the result is something like this:

```
          XOR A              clear the accumulator ('A')
          LD B,52            set a counter ('B')
          LD HL,WEEK1        set pointer to first figure
LOOP:     ADD A,(HL)         add the data pointed to by HL to the
                             accumulator
          INC HL             move the pointer up one
          DEC B              decrement counter
          JPNZ,LOOP          go round again if counter not zero
          LD(TOTAL),A        move the result to TOTAL
```

Again I am assuming that at some stage it is told where it can find WEEK1, and where it should put TOTAL.

What started as a nice straightforward job of adding up a few numbers has turned into eight separate operations, half of them being done 52 times each, none of them obviously relevant to the problem. Imagine trying to write a market-forecasting program in a language that takes eight statements to add up one lot of figures! All right; now imagine trying to maintain it!!

In the computer industry a need perceived has tended to mean a need satisfied, and it was not long before our little problem looked more like this:

```
TOTAL = 0;
DO I = 1 TO 52;
TOTAL = TOTAL + SALES (I);
END;
```

which is roughly the level computer language reached 20 years ago, and where it has remained ever since. It is the sort of thing programmers have come to expect: an accumulator is cleared; a control structure is defined which sets, then increments, a counter; each value is added in turn into the accumulator. In fact it is doing exactly what the assembler programs did, which is not too surprising since it will sooner or later be compiled into something virtually identical. However, eight pretty meaning-less statements have been replaced by two intelligible ones and one control structure, and at not too great a cost in efficiency. The high-level languages struck a balance between man and machine: the programmer was used many times more efficiently and the computer only slightly less so. The surprising thing is that the equilibrium has held for so long, and that it is only now being broken by something which was never designed as a computer language in the first place!

In APL, the solution to the problem would be

```
TOTAL←+/SALES
```

No control structure; no accumulator to clear; no mention of how many numbers there are to be added up. Just a straight statement of what is required: TOTAL is to be given the sum of all the numbers in SALES. No wonder it comes as a bit of a shock to someone who's spent his working life with a conventional computer language! The odd thing is that although APL is far quicker to program than, say, COBOL, it also makes pretty efficient use of the computer. It doesn't just tip the scales in the balance between man and machine; it actually moves the knife-edge right out of the programming department and into the world of the systems analyst.

The high-level languages were only one element in the computer industry's struggle to make better use of its programmers. The other was the foundation and development of Systems Analysis. To see how and why this came about I propose to take another look into the past, starting with some aspects of the commercial systems which were (and in some cases still are) written in assembly language. These were almost exclusively automated versions of existing clerical jobs: things like wages and invoicing where legions of clerks were employed to do simple, repetitive, easily codified tasks. The early computers with their assembler systems became the machine-tools of the clerical world. They were undoubtedly fast and efficient, and they replaced many jobs, but some of the other characteristics of the machine-tool came too and these were less well received. For a start they were very expensive so they had to be worked 24 hours a day to get value for money. Then companies found they needed a surprising number of highly trained specialists to drive their new machines, and they began to discover one or two fundamental truths about the developing art of computer programming.

To write really good assembler requires a very special kind of mental discipline and application. Even in rather simple programs it is all too easy to forget to clear the odd accumulator here, or set the occasional pointer there; and so, hardly were the first primitive systems out of the egg when the first program bugs began to appear. Companies who had just enough programmers to keep new systems coming suddenly found that they needed as many again to debug the systems they already had. Then, to add insult to injury, the company's requirements might change, and the programs had to be amended to match.

At this point these early systems had nearly reached the end of the road, because there is a pretty strict limit to the number of times you can patch an assembler program and still have any reasonable expectation of it continuing to function. So what were companies getting from this first generation of clerical machine-tool? On the plus side efficient, labour-saving clerical operations; on the minus side an expensive piece of equipment which needed specialists to run it, and which was not flexible enough to adapt to changing needs.

By taking away all the mundane tasks needed to program at the machine level, the high-level language obviously increased a programmer's productivity enormously: but it could not solve the problems unaided. The other vital element was the birth of Systems Analysis. What the systems analyst did was to break down the original problem into logical units which corresponded to processes the computer could handle. Because it could only read information in a rather limited number of ways (usually 80-column cards in the old days) some form of data preparation was needed; bits of paper with abbreviated scribbles were fine for the clerks, but had to be rigorously codified and neatly transcribed before they were fit for the computer to see. Then, of course, all this data had to be carefully checked and stored away somewhere. It could then be sorted, merged with other data, stored away somewhere else, processed in all sorts of ways, finally to emerge on to paper as the output from the system.

The benefits of breaking a system down this way were numerous: each of the units could be tested separately before being linked together; a small fault in one section could be trapped before it did any damage; and future change could be allowed for by isolating those parts of the system most liable to alter.

There were, however, some drawbacks. Each link in the chain meant a program, and before any of these programs could be written the programmer needed to know: what information was coming in; what the program had to do with it; how it was to be passed out. Consequently he could not really start programming until the whole system was designed down to the final detail, and the last thing he wanted was a change in the design half-way through. These constraints lead inexorably to the classical methods of systems analysis, followed by computer departments the world over:

- First, define the problem: make absolutely sure that you know exactly what your clients want, and what information you need to give it to them.

- Second, analyse the problem: break it down into steps a computer can cope with; make the basic information available as input data and decide how the output data is to be presented.

- Third, program and test all the individual steps and put them together to form the solution.

- Fourth, document the solution thoroughly, present the results to the client, and hand over the finished system to the operations department for day-to-day running.

When this method was first devised, the systems it was applied to were by and large well understood, logically organized clerical processes. Accountancy, for example, follows a series of strict rules which have been known for centuries; all the analyst needed to do to turn these into a workable computer system was a bit of transcription. Likewise payroll, sales ledger, inventory control: although less formalized the rules were well established and, equally important, they were not likely to change suddenly. In short these were ideal candidates for the design method that had grown up around them! Unfortunately for the developing computer industry, the supply of conveniently predigested problems was not inexhaustible. As the influence of the new design method spread deeper into company systems it was increasingly faced by tasks which were less well defined, and more liable to unexpected change; in fact it found itself out of its depth. To see what I mean, take the (apocryphal) story of a keen young analyst who is told to go away and computerize part of a typical company planning system.

Contrary to popular belief, the planning and control procedures of most companies are not neatly organized into a set of rational decisions taken on the basis of smoothly flowing information. Instead they have developed through a series of historical accidents, have little obvious logical structure, and such rules as they do have are riddled with exceptions. When the analyst applies his tried and trusted methods to these areas, a possible recipe for disaster goes something like this:

- *Defining the problem.* The analyst spends many happy weeks tracing information flows and interviewing all and sundry in the planning department. At the end of this time he has a perfectly clear picture of how the department is supposed to work; because this is how everyone in it has told him it works. Perhaps they even believe it; more commonly they just say the things best calculated to stop him asking awkward questions. Anyway, he can now confidently proceed to stage 2 . . . .

- *Analysing the problem.* This will take several months, by the end of which time the planning department will have long given up hope of ever seeing that nice young man again.

- *Programming the solution.* Assuming the analyst has made a good job of stage 2, it should not take longer than three or four months to program and test his system. By this time the planning department are either thoroughly cheesed off, or have given the whole idea up for lost.

- *Implementing the solution.* The analyst books a conference room for the day, lays on coffee and biscuits and delivers to the senior members of the planning area a beautifully professional presentation of the benefits of his system. They consume his coffee and nod wisely . . . .

What do these wise nods actually mean, and what will the future of the system be? Here are four possibilities; you can probably invent several more! To take the worst case first: the nods may imply full agreement with everything the analyst says. The system is then imposed from above by the planning manager and his clerks are told to make it work. Since the system will probably have little relevance to the way their job is actually done it may not impede them a great deal. The input will be given the minimum of thought and the output will quietly proceed to the waste-basket without getting in anybody's way. Of course if the manager actually *insists* on their using the system quite a lot of damage may be done before the whole project is abandoned amid endless recriminations. The resulting bad blood between the manager, his clerks, and the computer department may last for years.

A second possibility is that the managers have enjoyed the coffee, but failed to understand a word of the presentation. This is much less damaging, as although they will certainly adopt the system, their future interest in it will be confined to its value in impressing visiting directors. It will, indeed, fulfil this function quite admirably, as no director is liable to spot that most of the master files are several years out of date and that no-one actually seems to be using the system any more. However, no actual harm has been done to the company's operations, and the planning and computer departments at least remain on speaking terms.

A third possibility is that the planners have a pretty shrewd notion that something is not quite right, but, having been sufficiently doped with coffee and blinded with science, lack the confidence to say so. Of course they will not actually accept the system and the computer department may well waste a lot of time and energy trying to find out why; but all in all this seems the best outcome of the three. The potential for future co-operation between the planning and computer departments remains, and the only hurt feelings are those of the analyst. He can at least comfort himself with the knowledge that he did everything right!

Of course there is a fourth possibility: the analyst's view of the process may correspond sufficiently closely with reality that his system will function and will produce useful results. Unfortunately this is not the end of the story; in defining and analysing the problem he has perforce imposed upon the planners' world a structure of which they are not aware. When change comes to the system it may, if the analyst is lucky, fall within his defined structure; but there is absolutely no reason why it should. If it does not then nothing short of a total re-design will keep the system going, and no computer department can afford too many of those!

To recap then; in order to make better use of its precious programmers the computer industry came up with two things: the high-level language and Systems Analysis. This combination has successfully tackled a wide range of business problems, but can also fail disastrously when applied to areas for which it was never designed. Where then does APL fit into the picture? My basic thesis goes as follows: APL was designed as a way for people to communicate with each other, not as a means of instructing computers. It allows us to talk to them on our terms, hence it is inherently a more suitable tool for programming systems where the interaction between man and machine is paramount. In addition, the sheer speed with which it can be coded makes the whole carefully constructed edifice of user–analyst–programmer obsolete; indeed the extra line of communication may often be a positive handicap. Either analysts do not need programmers to do their donkey-work, or programmers do not need analysts to predigest the user's requests!

Whichever side you view it from, the relationship becomes meaningless. From now on, I shall try to use terms like 'system designer' and 'programmer' interchangeably to imply people who create and build computer systems; not to refer to different levels in a hierarchy.

I would like to round off this chapter with a story I heard recently of a group of programmers who won the right to join a particular union because '. . . they do not take decisions, and do not exercise management responsibility'. I fear that if their company ever adopts APL, the programmers may well be forced to leave that union! More seriously, I do believe that the social distinction which has built up between analysts – who give orders, and programmers – who take them, may significantly inhibit the development of APL in big companies. In particular it places a terrible handicap on those who would follow the philosophy expounded in Chapter 2 – design by evolution.

Chapter 2

Design by evolution – where and why?

'Managers do not solve problems; they manage messes.'
(Ackoff)

This chapter is not about APL as such, but about the design philosophy that under-pins much of the rest of this book. It is not easy for me to give hard and fast reasons why I feel that evolution will often succeed where analysis fails; basically my belief is a pragmatic one – I write systems this way, they get implemented, and they work. However, as a starting point, here is another version of the tale of the keen young analyst whom we left feeling so despondent in Chapter 1.

- *Stage 1.* He spends a few days in the planning office talking to anyone who has the time to see him. By doing this he both gets to know the people, and identifies a few simple needs that a computer could satisfy.

- *Stage 2.* He takes another couple of days to knock together some simple utilities, which, although pretty basic, can be hooked together to produce a system which actually helps the planners in their day-to-day work. Of course he doesn't bother about flashy VDU layouts or elegant reports; nor does he mind too much if the system falls over the first time someone enters some-thing unexpected.

- *Stage 3.* He moves a terminal into the planning office for a day, explains what he's done so far, and gives the planners a quick demonstration of the pro-grams. Their first reaction will probably be astonishment that anything, however primitive, could possibly be working so soon. Having spent an hour or so playing with it, they will get over their initial euphoria, and will start saying things like: 'I know I said . . . but what we really do is . . . ' or '. . . couldn't we use this for . . . ' or '. . . yes, that will work fine until . . . '. With a bit of luck the analyst will be able to make quite a lot of changes on the spot; he may even suggest some possibilities the planners themselves haven't thought of. By the end of the afternoon his major problem is liable to be res-cuing the terminal from the planning office!

- *Stage 4.* He now knows enough about the planning process to be able to re-write the initial draft into a reasonably robust first system. This will largely consist of the utilities he wrote for Stage 3, hidden under a bit of dialogue. It can, of course, be given piecemeal to the planners, and the design need never be totally fixed.

By the time Stage 4 is installed this approach has gone some way towards regaining the confidence of the planning management, and it has secured the active co-operation of the planners in developing the system further. This time what the analyst has done is to lay the foundations of a successful symbiosis between the computer's number-crunching power and the planner's lifetime of experience. As time goes on the planner will gradually change his way of working to make better use of the programs he has been given. At each change new horizons will open up, until the point is suddenly reached where a (computer-assisted) clerical job has become a genuine partnership between man and machine. Although the system will continue to evolve indefinitely into the future, at this point the analyst can certainly chalk up a successful implementation.

At this stage you may be asking: if this evolutionary approach is so marvellous, why have we been wasting all these years doing systems analysis? One answer is that until recently the tools to do evolutionary design (i.e. interactive computing, and especially APL) have been either unavailable or terribly expensive. Another is that it's very much a case of horses for courses: systematic design will always dominate in the world of large, stable systems. It's just that most of these (in big companies anyway) have already been done; the pressure for new developments is coming increasingly from areas much more suited to APL and the analyst-programmer.

Incidentally classical Systems is not the only discipline to be feeling the wind of change. For many years the practitioners of Operational Research (OR) (among whom I number myself) have been building increasingly sophisticated models and using them to solve company problems. To see which way OR is moving, here is a bit more of Professor Ackoff's address to the 1978 UK Conference.

'Managers are not confronted with static problems that are independent of each other, but with dynamic situations that consist of complex systems of changing problems that interact with each other. I call such situations *messes*. Problems are abstractions extracted from messes by analysis. . . .'

'Because messes are systems of problems, the sum of the optimal solutions to each component problem taken separately is *not* an optimal solution to the mess as a whole. The behaviour of a mess depends more on how the solutions to its parts *interact* than on how they act independently of one another.'

'Effective management of messes requires *planning*, not problem solving . . . . Planning and design are predominantly synthesizing, rather than analytic, activities; they involve putting things together rather than taking them apart. Moreover there is no such thing as an optimal plan for, or design of a purposeful system in a dynamic environment. The objective of such efforts should be to produce systems that can pursue ideals effectively and in a way that provides continuing satisfaction to the participants.'

Just as the classical methods of systems analysis have lost their way in the jungle of planning systems, so have the classical dogmas of OR! The remarkable thing is

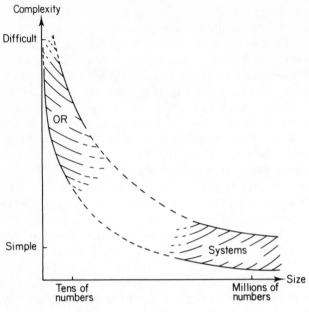

Figure 2.1

that having entered the maze with totally different prejudices, practitioners of both disciplines are reaching very similar conclusions about what needs to be done. To see why this is, I first want to talk a little bit more about the maze; how they got into it, and why something rather strange may happen in the middle! See Figure 2.1.

It seems to me that any computer system can be characterized by two main variables – size and complexity – and that by using these as the axes of a graph one can effectively map the traditional domains of Operational Research and Systems Analysis. So, up in the top left of Figure 2.1 we have classical OR, where tiny amounts of data are subjected to incredibly clever algorithms. Possibly an extreme example is a program I wrote a few years ago which works out the best pallet-layout for a box of a given size. The data input is literally three numbers; the program is over 500 lines of pretty terse PL/1! More typical might be the well known 'travelling salesman' problem, where the data consists simply of the coordinates of 40 or 50 calls; the programs to find the salesman's best route form a specialized branch even within OR!

So to the other end of the chart, wherein reside the thundering great DP systems beloved of the systems analyst. Mounds and mounds of data to be channelled through an easily defined sequence of nice, simple processes. To see what happens in the middle, I want to redraw Figure 2.1 in three dimensions, plotting vertically the transition from the systematic approach of the systems man to the analytical approach of the OR man (Figure 2.2).

The first, and most obvious question is: why have I drawn the surface with a fold? Again it's a subjective view, but I believe that for medium-size, reasonably complex 'messes' there is no middle ground. To see why, I'm going to start with a

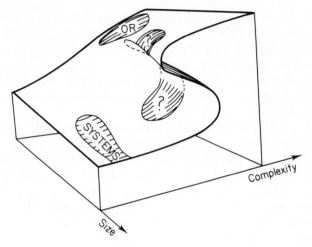

Figure 2.2

rather trivial example: how would each discipline design a system to play noughts and crosses (tic-tac-toe)? The analogue to the OR approach would be to take the position as it stood, e.g.

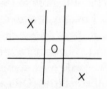

and to use a set of rules to work out where to play next. This would use a tiny amount of storage (basically nine numbers), and a pretty small, but by no means insignificant, amount of program.

The analogue to the systems approach would simply be to store all the possible games of noughts and crosses, and to flag any positions which were known to lead to a loss. The program to avoid these positions is trivial, and for such a small game no vast amount of storage would be needed either (there are only 77 distinct nought-has-won positions). From noughts and crosses we could move one of two ways: up into games with increasingly complex rules but still with rather low subtlety (e.g. boxed board games); or across into very large games with very simple rules (e.g. the Japanese game of Go). Now no one has yet solved Go, but there is no reason in principle why it should not be done. It's just that in practice the total number of possible games vastly exceeds the capacity of any conceivable computer memory! No, the real conceptual problem is the games that fall slap in the middle, chess being the classic example. Again it's too big to solve by brute force, but it's also complex enough that one cannot set any hard and fast rules which will select the 'best' move in any position. In other words it cannot be tackled either from the OR or from the systems viewpoint! The way such games are being approached is,

I believe, very instructive when it comes to systems for 'managing messes'. To play a reasonable game of chess a computer must have a dictionary of patterns (not of positions), a strategy based on advice (not particular moves), and a set of goals towards which the advice should eventually lead it. Now there is no doubt that many computers play more than just a reasonable game of chess, so why can't this approach be tried with the analogue to such games, i.e. the systems for planning and information?

The key lies in the fact that, unlike systems which play chess, planning systems must deal with a changing world; in particular the goals that they are seeking rarely stay constant for long. The OR approach, which is to make the model ever more complex, will always lag behind the problem it is trying to solve; the systems approach will be swamped by its own data.

To illustrate the point, I want to take another analogy, I hope not too far fetched: suppose military power A wants to drop something nasty on a target deep in the territory of military power B.

The OR solution is essentially ballistic: a complex model of the flight-path is devised, a solution (i.e. trajectory) is computed, the missile is pointed in the right direction and fired. At the opposite extreme is the cruise missile, which is provided with a detailed map of a narrow corridor of enemy terrain, and sent out to find its way along this. The OR method is clearly vulnerable to the unexpected, e.g. a sudden thunderstorm in its flight-path, but, more to the point, neither alternative has a hope of hitting a moving target! The only way to do that is to send in a piloted aircraft with some reasonably good maps, a decent navigation system, and a pilot who understands the target's behaviour. If, for 'navigation' and 'maps' you read 'planning' and 'information', then the analogy is complete. What is clear is that however accurate the trajectory of the ballistic (OR) approach, and however detailed the map of the cruise (systems) approach, there are some targets that neither will reach. To hit these you must abandon both methods, and should concentrate your efforts on developing good maps and sophisticated aids to navigation, and on training your pilots to use them.

What it all comes down to is that we still need people: people with the experience to perceive the patterns, with the expertise to use the advice, with the sensitivity to adapt to a changing world. Because we (the analysts) are in the business of providing tools for such people to use, we must first understand how their job is done before we can even begin. The trouble is that the tools we provide will radically change the job, and the tool users must be given time to adapt before they can start to suggest improvements. Impasse! Such systems cannot be broken down into problems which the OR man can analyse; all we can do is to start somewhere and let the system grow.

To look at the same thing from another viewpoint: both classical OR and standard analysis aim to produce systems which will *replace* man as a decision-taker. In the pallet-layout example I quoted earlier, the object of the exercise was to produce layouts which were *better* than those issued by the company's product development department. In such diverse areas as inventory control and payroll, computer systems have taken over from people as the authority which determines when orders are sent out, and when wages are paid. Much publicity is occasioned when either approach fails, but there is no doubt that for the two extremes (complex data/simple process; simple data/complex process) computers can and do replace people effectively. It is into the much more woolly areas of planning and control that computer technology is spreading, and here the emphasis is on decision support, not decision taking.

The system takes care of the routine tasks, and presents the planner with information in the way best calculated to help him use his subjective judgment. This both gives him more time to deal with the frequent minor crises, and improves the chance that he will act correctly to resolve them. Surely it must by now be self-evident that a system such as this cannot be designed from scratch. Even the obvious first stage of automating the more straightforward of the planning tasks will radically alter the planner's approach to his job. Any attempt to define his information needs in detail must wait until he has adjusted his way of working to take advantage of Stage 1. Even then, the process is largely one of trial and error, of trying out prototypes and following up promising leads.

There I rest my case for evolutionary design. I hope I haven't given the impression that it is a sort of fall-back, to be used when all else fails; it has a lot of other points in its favour, and I shall try to list a few of them. First, there's the psychological benefit for the user; people really do care about the systems that form such a big part of their working lives. What better way to fulfil this need than to involve them in the design – possibly even in the programming – of the system right from the start? Secondly, an evolving system will start to pay back its costs almost immediately. In stringent economic times companies just cannot afford a two-year time lapse before a new system begins to pay its way. Thirdly, you simply get better systems! I know that's little more than a personal statement of faith, but I hope the rest of this chapter has provided enough argument to convince those who treat such bold claims with justified scepticism.

In summary then, when faced with a complex tangle of problems in a changing world the analyst has only one realistic choice: evolution. Later on I want to develop the methodology of evolutionary design a lot further, but before that I must take some time off to talk about APL. I want to say why I think APL is particularly appropriate to this sort of system, and to give some hints on how it should be written if its unique characteristics are to be used to best advantage.

Chapter 3

Why APL?

Just what is so special about APL? Why is it that gatherings of APL devotees have an atmosphere akin to religious revival meetings? On the other hand why do many DP managers view 'in-house' APL with such deep suspicion, and is there any basis for their fears? These are the sort of questions I want to look at in this chapter, I hope dispassionately! First, I'll take some of APL's strong points, in particular those most relevant to the evolutionary approach. Then I must restore the balance by admitting to some of the problems you may well encounter. Finally, for those who decide that APL really is for them – some of the pros and cons in the 'bureau versus in-house' debate.

APL gives the programmer two tools which no traditional language can offer: a working environment in which program and data co-exist on an equal footing; and a consistent and powerful notation with which to manipulate them. Most planning (and many information) systems fall in the middle ground where the interaction between programs and data can be extremely complex; APL, with its 'workspace' concept, makes light of the subtlest interdependencies.

This interchangeability of programs and data can be immensely helpful when you are first putting an application together; for example you might start with

```
SALESPLAN←?10 12ρ100
```

and use these randomly generated figures to test a series of functions in a production scheduling system. When the algorithm is working to your satisfaction, you want to switch to the real figures which are stored externally on a file. To do this, you simply define a function:

```
    SALES←SALESPLAN
    ---------------

[1]   ⍝READ SALES DATA FROM FILE.

[2]     SALES← .......
      ∇
```

and all your planning functions will continue to execute as if nothing had happened.

Planning systems also tend to need a fair amount of abstract modelling, which is just what 'Iverson's Notation' was designed for. Before this ever became APL it was in use the world over as a concise, consistent way of expressing technical algorithms. The first APL interpreters simply relieved the early practitioners of the burden of translating their algorithms into a conventional language! I can't resist throwing in

16

an example from my own experience: my problem was a subroutine to take a string of numbers and return the same list shuffled. In PL/1 (I won't bore you with the gory details) this took a couple of loops and 22 statements; in APL the whole thing collapsed into

```
RESULT←LIST[(ρLIST)?ρLIST]
```

Can you wonder that I haven't written much PL/1 since?!

The sheer conciseness of APL has the additional advantage that it simply takes less time to code it, and this can be important when you're changing a program with the user at your elbow. In fact it makes the whole business of 'programming by negotiation' (of which more in Chapter 6) feasible. The fact that APL is genuinely interactive helps too; to be able to alter programs 'in flight', and to try out bits of code at the terminal, is an enormous boon when you need results quickly. Add to this APL's superbly general functional structure, its steadily improving file-handling and its recent acquisition of full-screen management, and the question becomes 'why not APL?'.

Having spent a page or so extolling the virtues of APL, I must now restore the balance by admitting to a few of the drawbacks. Once again the problem lies in trading off the cost of hardware against software, but the balance is by no means as clear-cut as it first appears. Efficiency is one of the more contentious issues; many DP departments still live in fear of a couple of APL terminals bringing the whole system to a grinding halt. They are often right, but for all the wrong reasons! The myth goes that interpreters are slower than compilers, therefore APL (being interpreted) will take more CPU to do the same job than, say, FORTRAN. For normal computer languages the conclusion holds, but (as I keep saying) APL is not a normal computer language. It has an enormously powerful syntax, but the only symbols which may change the order in which code is executed are '→' and '()'. This makes the job of turning a line of APL into machine code relatively straightforward; and, because each operator does a clearly defined job, that machine code can be optimized so that it runs very fast indeed. What can slow APL down is its dynamic management of storage; this may sometimes be a severe burden, but it is hardly a direct result of interpretation! In fact, as interpreters get steadily cleverer, even this is becoming much less of a handicap in the comparison with conventional languages. My experience is that a well thought out, well written APL system will use just about the same amount of machine resource, on average, as the same system written in a conventional language.

The reason for this is straightforward enough: every time a PL/1 program is changed, however trivially, at least a substantial chunk of it must be recompiled. In APL, on the other hand, the only parts of the program the interpreter sees are the bits that are actually in use! Vast tracts of code, usually error routines and the like, may never get interpreted at all once the system has gone 'live'. Consequently, it doesn't take a particularly high inflow of minor changes to leave the APL system ahead in the CPU stakes, and APL systems have been justified on the CPU savings alone. Even leaving this point aside, it is quite possible to concoct tests whereby an

APL function will perform the same task faster than compiled, optimized PL/1! Not remotely typical, I know, but intriguing all the same.

Of course the 'machine costs' of a system are declining rapidly in comparison with the 'people costs', and one of the joys of APL is that it gives a system manager some control over where the balance is to be struck. This choice again arises from APL's ability to regard programs as data, and vice versa. You can create a whole range of software aids, written in APL, to help you with the development, maintenance, and documentation of your APL systems. Examples would include full-screen function editing, global search-and-replace for a given name, automatic production of function listings, and cross-reference tables. Such aids, particularly the 'document' functions, contribute large savings in programmer time, but tend to make correspondingly heavy demands on the CPU. By regulating their use (e.g. workspace documentation only after 5.00 p.m. or during the lunch hour), an APL installation can effectively 'fine-tune' the trade-off between its programmers and its hardware.

Why then have I said that DP departments are right to be afraid of APL? I can find two of the answers in the discussion above: the key phrases are 'well written' and 'on average'. It is very hard indeed to write **FORTRAN** or PL/1 sufficiently badly to produce any noticeable drop in efficiency; the same is not true of APL, where two different ways of coding the same problem may easily differ in speed by a factor of a hundred! For example, both the expressions below will take a numeric vector and turn it into a one-column matrix:

```
V←1000ρ10

M←((ρV),1)ρV          2 ms

M←V∘.+,0              115 ms
```

Possibly an extreme example, but on the face of it there is absolutely nothing wrong with the second expression; it just happens to take 50 times as long as the first! An interesting piece of evidence for the dangers of thoughtless programming comes from a recent IBM research report (Waldbaum, 1978). This includes several fascinating case studies of desperately (and unnecessarily) inefficient programs, but from my point of view the most interesting figures are the percentages of users who managed to absorb half of the prime-shift CPU time. On OS it took around 4% of the users to consume 50% of the available CPU; on VM/370 between 3% and 4%; on APLSV the figure was 1%! Aberrant behaviour in APL can cause far more damage to a computer system than the grossest misuse of conventional language.

Having accepted that inefficiently written APL can consume far more than its fair share of precious CPU – what's wrong with *good* APL? The problem lies in the nature of the load that a typical clutch of APL applications creates. Today's big mainframes tend to be built around the traditional batch job stream: a job comes in, occupies an area of storage which doesn't fluctuate too much, takes a steady ration of the CPU cycles, and goes away, only to be replaced by another job of largely similar characteristics. Throw in a couple of APL systems, and this pleasantly ordered flow may develop some rather drastic turbulence! It's not that the APL load *per se* is particularly heavy, it's just rather difficult to mix it sensibly with an existing batch schedule.

DP trepidation at the idea of a mixed batch–APL load is not without foundation after all!

So far all the discussion is this chapter has assumed that there is a simple choice between an APL system and a system written along conventional lines. Of course life is rarely as simple as that; most companies already have an enormous invest-ment in conventionally structured data. Whether sequential, random access or data-base, such data is always designed to be used an element at a time; if this is to be accessed by an APL system there are two ways of doing it, but neither is particu-larly satisfactory. For example, suppose APL is being considered for a system to query a company's personnel records. At first sight it is the ideal vehicle for such a system: to answer questions like

```
AVERAGE SALARY WHERE AGE>35
```

all that is needed is a couple of APL vectors (SALARY and AGE) and two one-line functions (AVERAGE and WHERE). The problem is in creating these vectors; Figure 3.1 shows what I mean.

Conventional data format

Employee	Salary	Age
2501	10005	46
2503	7896	27
2504	12487	51
.	.	.
.	.	.
.	.	.

APL data format

Employee	...	...	...	2501 2503 2504	...	...
Salary	...	...	...	10005 7896 12487	...	...
Age	...	...	...	46 27 51	...	...

Figure 3.1

The first possibility is to forgo the elegance of parallel processing and to use APL to read the conventional file a record at a time. If the company had no more than a few hundred employees this might be a reasonable way out; more than this and the overhead of interpreting the same piece of code several thousand times becomes too severe. The other approach is to design a batch conversion program which effectively 'inverts' the personnel file.

Of course this is rather wasteful of storage and the file inversion may take a significant amount of CPU time, but it does leave the data in a format which APL can process very efficiently. (The subject of file inversion does get a section to itself later on in Chapter 12.) This method only really makes sense for quite slow-moving data; weekly or even monthly inversions may suffice for the personnel system, but the prospect of daily inversions of more volatile data is not one that the DP department will view with pleasure.

I hope this chapter has demonstrated that there is often no clear-cut answer to the question 'why APL?'. It is a problem-solving tool of quite unique capabilities, but it is not the answer to everything. As a summary of a few of the pros and cons, here are some candidates for the APL approach, with comments on each.

System	Why APL	Why not APL
A quick 'one-off'	Will get results in days rather than weeks	May be rather expensive, and 'one-offs' have a nasty habit of becoming permanent
A complex file-query system	Query language is easy to build and quick to modify	Overhead of inversion; limit of workspace size
A complex planning job which uses little or no external data	Faster, more concise, and more flexible than any conventional language	May cause system programmers a few headaches
Any prototype system	Gets the bugs out of the design at very little cost; can be used as the specification for the real system	Again there is a danger of it becoming permanent
A large and repetitive data-cruncher, e.g. payroll, simulation, linear programming	May be the only way to get something off the ground fast enough	Very expensive

You can, of course, bypass many of the problems by running your APL system on a time-sharing bureau; this is certainly one of the commonest ways to get started. Many companies move their APL in-house sooner or later, simply on the grounds of cost, but doing your work over the phone line does have its advantages, for example:

- The service is usually guaranteed 24 hours a day, seven days a week. Bureaux live or die by response times; this may well be better than an in-house service will give.

- The communications are done for you; if you have a couple of hundred branch offices around the world it is very handy to let them share a common database for the cost of a telephone call to the nearest node in the bureau's network.

- Most bureaux leave lots of useful data/utility functions lying around for you to use. They also provide 'free' advice (and education) for novice users.

- The APL itself may be better – APL*PLUS is rather more powerful than anything IBM currently offer. However, this is rather a double-edged sword – stay too long on the bureau and it may be very difficult to break away!

Why, then, run APL in-house? Cost is one reason I've already mentioned; some others are as follows:

- The considerable hassle of proofing all your systems against 'line-drops'. Even if a total loss of telephone line is uncommon, there is nothing more irritating to a user than a sudden splurge of noise in the middle of an other-wise neat report.

- Sooner or later you'll want to get at company data with your APL system. Copying the relevant files to tape and shipping them to the bureau is rarely a satisfactory solution; there is just too much scope for administrative error!

- Many users insist that their data is too sensitive to be allowed off the premises anyway.

- APL is moving rapidly from the teletype age into the VDU age. Even over a good leased line, much of the advantage of the screen may be lost when it is used remotely. However, as line speeds increase, and VDUs get cleverer, this problem could recede quite quickly.

All of which assumes that you want to use APL in the first place! I hope this chapter has at least gone some way towards answering the questions I posed at the start. I hope also that I have pointed out some of the problems you may find, whether you run your APL on your own computer or decide to use a time-sharing bureau. Whichever you choose, if you have found a satisfactory answer to 'Why APL?' then the next logical question is 'How?'. The answer to that one forms the rest of this book.

Chapter 4

Structure and style in APL

This is not in any way, shape, or form an attempt to lay down standards; better men than I have perished in that mine-field. Instead I have assembled a collection of advice, anecdotes, and examples which you can take or leave as you wish. The material is not laid out in any particular order, but I have tried to make each section as self-contained as possible. The topics covered in this chapter are:

> Aims and objectives
> Idioms in APL
> Linking functions together
> Useful ways of doing nothing
> To loop or not to loop
> Recursed!
> The user's view: closed versus open systems
> How much code on one line?
> Zero-origin – pros and cons
> Ways of branching, and IF functions
> Some thoughts on structured programming
> Ways of looping, if you have to

In general, I have tried to suppress personal prejudices; I hope the text makes it reasonably clear where I have failed!

Aims and Objectives

To what should the APL programmer aspire? To the most elegant use of the language? To the most efficient code? To the most flexible and easily maintained system? Perhaps just to get results in the shortest possible time?! It all depends on the context, who is to use the programs and how. Let me take the four aspirations above, and try to give a context for each.

   To make the most elegant use of the language. Always valid, but not at the expense of the other three. Elegance must be a personal judgment, and your 'elegant' code may not happen to be the most efficient, flexible, or fastest to write. If it is, you are lucky indeed, and this section need trouble you no further!

   To the most efficient code. Efficient in what sense – in its use of you or the machine? Probably the latter for utility functions which are heavily used and rarely altered; more likely the former for the top-level functions which will change constantly.

To the most flexible and easily maintained system. Yes, but don't spend too long designing it. This may conflict with efficiency too, especially in storing data.

To get the thing done. Political necessity is often enough to leave this the sole criterion by which the programmer is judged.

Idioms in APL

'It's raining cats and dogs!' we might exclaim (in Britain anyway!), meaning that rain is presently falling unusually heavily. No one actually reads the individual words in an idiom like that – the meaning is implicit in the phrase as a whole. Whether you are 'getting on like a house on fire' or preparing to 'turn over a new leaf', you certainly don't expect your listeners to take such phrases apart to appreciate their full meaning. On the contrary, much of the meaning may be lost if this is done!

APL is full of such idioms, and the same rules apply; for example

```
V[⍋V]
```

is not understood any better by taking it apart. On the contrary, it is very easy to appreciate 'sort V', whereas 'index V by its ascending grade' makes far less sense. The beauty of an idiomatic approach to APL is that once an idiom is learned it can be remembered thereafter as a unit, and recognized as such by others. Another example might be

```
<\bit vector
```

to leave only the left-most '1' switched on. The idiom '`<\`' is read as 'first occurrence of . . . ' and should be taught as such; the details of how it actually achieves this result merely confuse the issue!

There is, of course, one interesting sideline on the subject of idioms – dialect! If a Yorkshireman tells his wife that he 'won't be back while 9.00' he will be readily enough understood, and his supper will be on the table at 9.05. To anyone unfamiliar with this highly local usage of 'while' to mean 'until', the sentence is totally confusing. The same might well come to apply in APL, as the same basic language elements are put together in different ways by different groups of programmers. For example to strip trailing blanks from a character-string one might one day come across

```
STRING←(⌽v\⌽STRING≠' ')/STRING
```

and on another day

```
STRING←(1-(STRING=' ')⍳1)↓STRING
```

Both versions are equally valid and each will be read with equal facility as 'chop off trailing blanks' by their respective programmers. The problems, as with the Yorkshire 'while', come when one is faced with a program written in a very unfamiliar dialect. If you can't read the idioms, then trying to find out what a piece of APL code does really is no fun at all.

I suspect that the development of idioms is still at quite an early stage in the APL community; after all the notation has only been around for 10 years or so. However, there are already some nice examples of what one might call 'compound idioms'. For example, to remove duplicates from a vector one might use

```
VEC←(1 1 ⍉ <\VEC∘.=VEC)/VEC
```

This uses three idioms in all:

`<\`	we have already met
`1 1 ⍉`	major diagonal
`VEC←(..condition)/VEC`	sieve on given condition

to achieve the final idiom 'remove duplicates'. Of course you may also see

```
VEC←((VEC⍳VEC)=⍳⍴VEC)/VEC
```

and I'm sure there are many others!

For those of you who would like to see more of the idioms in current usage, there is a much more extensive collection in Chapter 8.

Linking Functions Together

Excluding clever things with shared variables, there are two basic ways of doing this.

Pseudo-primitives

These are functions which behave exactly like the APL symbols, i.e. they take one or two arguments and they return one result. They have no other effect on the environment whatsoever. Because they behave like the APL symbols, they can be strung together in the same way and the APL interpreter will sort out the syntax. For example

```
(ΔRJUST ΔALPHSORT ',' ΔTAB 'FRED,JOE,HARRY'),'!'


        FRED!
        HARRY!
         JOE!
```

(See Chapter 8 for the functions ΔRJUST, ΔALPHSORT and ΔTAB.)

Note that the following is not a pseudo-primitive:

```
      R←A PLUS B
      ----------
  [1]   R←A+B
  [2]   ΔFLG←1
        ∇
```

Line 2 disqualifies it!

Communication via global variables

This is common among the higher-level functions, since users may get confused by complex syntax, arguments and results. For example:

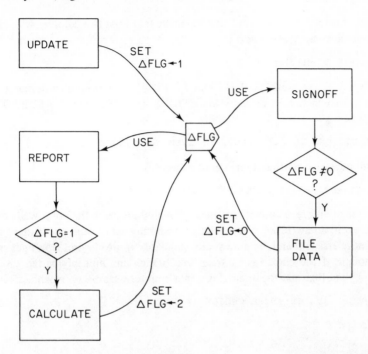

The user never sees ΔFLG, so he won't get confused, but he won't understand either, so he may beat the system by doing things in the wrong order! This approach also makes the system harder to maintain, because no state-using function can be fully understood without reference to all the state-setting functions. Moral: try for pseudo-primitives where you can; resort to globals where you must.

Useful Ways of Doing Nothing

Some typical ways of doing nothing:

```
VAR←VAR+0
VAR←VAR×1
VAR←0⌈VAR          (VAR is positive)
VAR←VAR,''         (VAR is a character vector)
⍃''
```

How can these be used to advantage? Here are a few examples.

• Add 1 to score if answer is right:

```
SCORE←SCORE+ANSWER=RIGHT
```

- Set all negative values in list to zero:

```
LIST←0⌈LIST
```

- Pad character matrix with blanks to make it at least five columns wide. If it is wider anyway, leave it as it is:

```
MAT←(0 5⌈ρMAT)↑MAT
```

- Display the message 'ADDITIONS TO FILE', unless the new item is a duplicate, in which case display 'ADDITIONS TO FILE; ITEM ALREADY ON FILE:

```
'ADDITIONS TO FILE',DUP/' : ITEM IS ALREADY ON FILE'
```

- Call new page routine if line count exceeds 65:

```
±(LINECT>65)/'LINECT←ΔNEWPAGE PC←PC+1'
```

There are many more examples, but these probably illustrate the point well enough. You can avoid an awful lot of branching by cunning use of 'null operations'; this is usually more efficient and, by almost any standards, more elegant. Don't get carried away though; if the choice is between one branch and multiplying ten thousand numbers by one then take the branch! Another counter-example is in menu-selections:

```
OPTION←ΔVALIN'ENTER CHOICE (1 TO 9) :- '
```

- *Method 1*

```
    →(L1,L2,....)[OPTION]
L1:REPORT1
    →EXIT
L2:REPORT2
    →EXIT
```

etc.

- *Method 2*

```
±(OPTION=1)/'REPORT1'
±(OPTION=2)/'REPORT2'
```

etc.

Method 2 may look a lot neater, but it is less efficient. Executing nothing eight times takes a lot longer than a couple of jumps! Of course if all the sub-functions are 'REPORT' suffixed by the option number, then

```
±'REPORT',⍕OPTION
```

is the best of the lot.

Note that all these ways round branching rather give the lie to the idea that flowcharts are language-independent. In APL a flowchart is usually just a vertically connected series of boxes!

One final thought on branch avoidance is to define 'null functions', e.g.

```
        R←FLG FN VALUE
        --------------

   [1]    ⍝DOES NOTHING IF FLG IS ZERO

   [2]    R←VALUE
   [3]    →FLG↓0
   [4]    ...............etc.
          ∇
```

This buries the branch inside FN, so that when it is called the code might look like

```
   FIGS←(ASK'CHECK THE DATA ?') FN ∆READIT 'DATAFILE'
```

which looks much clearer than the alternative of branching round FN if the answer is 'NO'.

To Loop or Not to Loop?

On the face of it a silly question. The interpretive overhead goes through the roof when looping code is executed. There are, however, times when looping can be more efficient; a classic example is in string searching. (Those of you lucky enough to use a version of APL with a ⎕SS function can ignore the next bit.) The sledge-hammer approach,

```
   POS←(∧≠(0,⍳⁻1+⍴SUB)⌽SUB∘.=TARGET)/⍳⍴TARGET
```

makes all possible matches of SUB against TARGET. Apart from the ever-present danger of WS FULL, most of these matches are unnecessary. The rather sophisticated ∆SS (see Chapter 8 for a listing) does loop, but can be several hundred times faster. It starts by looking for the character in SUB *least* likely to be found in TARGET, then only a few characters in TARGET (those in the right relative positions) need to be checked for the next least likely character, and so on. The extra work done by the interpreter is more than made up for by the saving in execution time.

The other time to loop is when the closed-form version is so complex or obscure that it takes half a day to get it working. This sort of mental effort is probably only justified for system utilities which are in very common use; otherwise it just isn't worth it. Remember: you are a more important resource than the computer!

Recursed!

What is it about recursion that makes me want to hide in a corner and whimper? Somehow the idea of a function: calling itself, calling itself . . . , and so on; then unwinding; then doing it again; eventually to emerge triumphant from its own intestines - is enough to give anyone the creeps!

There is all the difference in the world between when you can use recursion, and when you should:

28

- You *can* use it when you need to solve a problem which breaks down naturally into a series of smaller problems which look just like the big one. The process will continue until one of the smaller problems is trivial, when the whole process will go into reverse, and the recursion will unwind.

- You *should* use it when it is necessary for one of the sub-problems to refer back to the result of a previous step in the chain. This is very rare, except in some decidedly off-beat mathematics.

For an example of recursion in full flight see Chapter 10; for the moment I want to confine myself to a simple example which could equally (and more efficiently) have been defined with looping.

To add two binary numbers, using 'not equivalent' and 'carry':

```
      Z←A ADDER B;C
      -------------

[1]   ⍝BINARY ADDITION FROM FIRST PRINCIPLES.

[2]   Z←A≠B
[3]   →(∨/C←A∧B)↓0
[4]   Z←Z ADDER 1↓C,0
      ∇
```

The User's View: Closed versus Open Systems

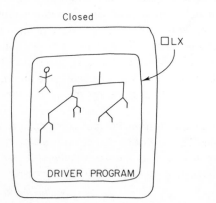

In a closed system, the user is always under control. He is given a choice of options, and may select only from those offered. Consequently he will never do anything silly, because you never give him the chance.

In an open system an initial WELCOME function releases the user straight back into APL. He can then use any of the functions available to him in any sequence whatsoever. (Of course WELCOME may set a flag somewhere to debar access to certain functions.) This approach has two main advantages over the closed system:

it allows the user to adapt his way of working without causing any programming changes; and it greatly reduces the total amount of coding needed to get the application going. Driver functions tend to be pretty wordy and very tedious to write. The open system has the disadvantage that an over-adventurous user can get himself into trouble, so the onus is on you to make sure he really understands the system.

Even if you eventually intend a system to be closed, you should always start off with an open system, and write the driver last.

How Much Code on One Line?

Even without the diamond separator you can get an absurd amount of code on one APL line. The string search a couple of pages back is by no means an extreme example, and many APL programmers seem to regard 'one-liners' as the ultimate achievement. There seem to be two reasons for this: in some very early APLs functions were read from disk a line at a time and the one-liner was thus a very efficient animal; the second reason is the simple intellectual challenge. Writing a complex piece of code in as few lines as possible is just like solving a crossword puzzle; indeed obscure code for the sake of it is a common enough phenomenon in conventional languages. It's just that APL gives the obscurantist more scope!

On the other hand, code can be over-simplified. Suppose we want to replace all the underscores in a vector by blanks; which of the following two versions is clearer? This

```
HITS←VEC='_'
LEN←ρVEC
POS←HITS/ιLEN
VEC[POS]←' '
```

or this

```
VEC[(VEC='_')/ιρVEC]←' '
```

Moral: each line of code should perform one logical operation, of the sort of complexity you could describe easily in one sentence. A good guideline is that if a statement gets deeper than three levels of brackets it's ripe for breaking up.

Zero-origin – Pros and Cons

Why have the option of counting from zero at all? I suspect that the main reason is historical: the early implementers of APL were all fluent assembler programmers, and assemblers all use zero-origin for things like memory offsets and table indices. Thus they often felt more comfortable counting 0, 1, 2, . . . than 1, 2, 3, . . . , so they gave themselves the option of doing so in APL. Of course once it was there people found all sorts of elegant uses for it: for example to set a flag to 'P' or 'T' in response to the question 'PRODUCTION OR TRIAL?'

```
∆TRL←'TP'['P'=1↑BAREIN'PRODUCTION OR TRIAL ? :- ']
```

is rather neater in zero-origin.

Also in graph-plotting, where you often end up with an array of zeros and ones, and want to display it, then

```
    GRAPH←' *'[MAT]
```
zero-origin

is a bit neater than

```
    GRAPH←' *'[1+MAT]
```
one-origin

The encode/decode functions work much more neatly in zero-origin too.

So much for the good points; now for some drawbacks. The first is that unless you are very sure of what you are doing zero-origin will sooner or later catch you out; for example a branch of the form

```
    →LAB×ιA>B
```

won't go to LAB at all in zero-origin, it will terminate the function!

The second reason is the overhead of making all your utility functions origin-independent. This more than makes up in messiness and obfuscation for all the elegance gained in the calling functions. Things like

```
    MAT←MAT,[□IO] LINE
```

take up unnecessary CPU time and look rather horrid. Not to mention the fact that you will have to test them all twice; once in one-origin, once in zero-origin. Of course you could always localize the index-origin, and reset it within each utility. Again it's messy, and again it wastes CPU time.

My personal feeling is that zero-origin is better forgotten about, but perhaps that's just because I find counting from zero a strange and unnatural habit! If you do use it, at least be aware of the problems.

Ways of Branching, and Some IF Functions

When it comes to conditional branching, APL provides the programmer with something of an embarrassment of riches. Many of the methods rely on the facts that: (a) a branch to a null vector is not a branch at all; (b) any arithmetic operation with a null vector is itself a null vector. For example

```
    →LABEL⌈ιA>B
    →LABEL×ιA>B
```

Others use compression to produce the desired null result:

```
    →(A>B)/LABEL
    →((A>B),(A<B),1)/GT,LT,EQ
```

This also relies on the fact that a branch to a vector (e.g. 5 6 7) in fact goes to the first label in the vector. Thus the conditions need not be mutually exclusive; if two or more are true, then the left-most is the one that determines the branch point.

This useful fact is also exploited in branch instructions such as

```
→( ..expression.. )φL1,L2,L3
```

Another property which comes in useful is the behaviour of take and drop on labels. The four possibilities are:

```
( ..positive number.. )↑LAB      LAB, 0 0 etc.
( ..ZERO ..            )↑LAB      null vector
( ..non-zero number.. )↓LAB      null vector
( ..ZERO ..            )↓LAB      LAB
```

which gives the very neat pairing of

```
→( ..expression.. )↑LABEL      branch if
→( ..expression.. )↓LABEL      branch if not
```

Note that the expression may evaluate to zero or one, in which case the first of these behaves identically to

```
→( ..condition.. )/LABEL
```

However, the version using take seems to be fractionally faster on most APL systems. (See Table 4.1 for the exact figures.)

Table 4.1   Relative times of some branch methods

Statement	Time for 100 executions (ms)
→8	1.2
→LAB	4.2
→C↑LAB	10
→C/LAB	12
→LAB×ιC	17
→LABΓιC	17
→LAB IF C	25
→LAB WHEN C	55

All the timings were on an IBM 3032, running VS APL under VSPC.
For comparison:
```
ค              1.1 ms
±0/'ABCDE' 18 ms
```

Finally, of course, there is nothing to stop you burying any of these in a function, and calling it IF. You can then write

```
→LABEL IF A>B
```

32

which must be the most readable of the lot. The simplest form of such functions is
just

```
      R←LAB IF COND
      -------------
[1]   R←COND↑LAB
      ▽
```

Another possibility is a function with the following properties:

→$\underline{L}$AB WHEN COND	true	goes to $\underline{L}$AB
	false	no branch
→($\underline{L}$1,$\underline{L}$2) WHEN COND	true	goes to $\underline{L}$1
	false	goes to $\underline{L}$2
→($\underline{L}$1,$\underline{L}$2) WHEN (COND1),COND2	$\underline{L}$1, $\underline{L}$2, or no branch	
→($\underline{L}$1,$\underline{L}$2,$\underline{L}$3) WHEN (COND1),COND2	$\underline{L}$1, $\underline{L}$2, or $\underline{L}$3 if neither	

etc., for as many labels as you like.

The second example has the great advantage of stating both branch points
explicitly. Even if one is redundant, this can add dramatically to the clarity of the
code. Incidentally, a similar convention was used in some very early FORTRANs
where the conditional statement was

IF (A > B) 1,2

which branched to 2 if the condition was true, otherwise to 1.

Anyway, if you want to use 'WHEN', here it is:

```
      R←LAB WHEN COND
      ---------------
[1]   R←(~(ρLAB)↑COND=0)/LAB
      ▽
```

Happy branching!

Some Thoughts on Structured Programming

The 'GOTO', it is often said, is the bane of the structured programmer's life. How
then dare I raise the subject in a book about APL, which knows no other way?
First, I would like to take issue with those who say that GOTOs, of themselves,
lead to 'spaghetti programs'; such code is the consequence of one thing only -
bad programming. What is true is that by banning GOTOs a language designer can
make it virtually impossible for you to write *really* convoluted code. In APL no
such safeguard exists, and the responsibility remains with the programmer; branches
round branches - this is the horror that the structured language keeps you from and
that you must consciously avoid in APL!

In theory you should be able to break down any programming task into some
combination of only three basic forms:

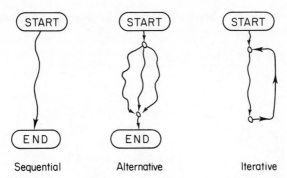

| | | Sequential | Alternative | Iterative |

In APL *sequential* is obviously the default; unless we do something to stop it line 5 will follow line 4 and line 6 will follow line 5.

The *alternative* structure can very often be achieved without an actual branch instruction (see 'Useful ways of doing nothing'); otherwise something like

SELECT...			
IF Condition 1	ORIF Condition 2	ORIF Condition 3	ELSE
PROCESS 1	PROCESS 2	PROCESS 3	PROCESS 4

```
→(L1,L2,L3,DEFLT) WHEN (CASE1),(CASE2),CASE3
```
or
```
→((CASE1),(CASE2),(CASE3),1)/L1,L2,L3,DEFLT
```
etc., represents this one neatly enough. Of course the 'IF-THEN' is really only a subset of this:

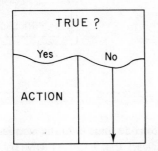

TRUE ?	
Yes	No
ACTION	

```
→(COND)↓SKIP
ACTION
SKIP:'READY'
```

What about *iterative* structures? Clearly the most important thing is the way we escape from them, and there are three possible places to get out: the top, the

34

bottom, and somewhere in between. Here are the three types, represented both in flowchart and block diagram style:

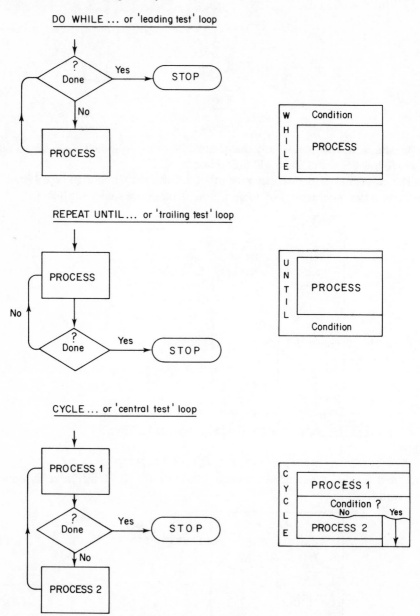

I'm going to leave the details of how to code these until the next section, but the structures themselves make one point clear: the 'REPEAT UNTIL' will do PROCESS at least once, come what may, whereas the 'DO WHILE' can gracefully do nothing.

Finally, an example of how the CYCLE and CASE structures might come together in an APL dialogue, this time in block-diagram form only:

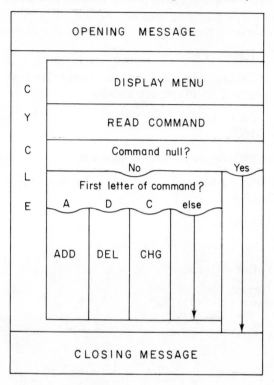

The APL code for this is

```
DIALOGUE;LAB;CMD
----------------

[1]      ⍝SAMPLE DIALOGUE FUNCTION

[2]       'UPDATE ROUTINE BEGINS'
[3]       LAB←ADD,DEL,CH,SKIP
[4]  MENU:→(ρCMD←BAREIN 'ENTER NEXT OPTION :- ')↓EXIT
[5]       →LAB['ADC'⍳1↑CMD]
[6]   ADD:ED∆ADD
[7]       →SKIP
[8]   DEL:ED∆DEL
[9]       →SKIP
[10]   CH:ED∆CH
[11] SKIP:→MENU
[12] EXIT:'END OF UPDATE ROUTINE'
      ∇
```

This may look obvious, but it does illustrate one important point: the branches on
lines 7 and 9 *must* go to the end of the CASE clause (i.e. S KIP), *not* back to the
menu. I know it's two branches instead of one, but it just isn't worth compro-
mising your principles to save that trivial an amount of CPU time!

Ways of Looping, if You Have To

Having decided that a loop is necessary, how should the APL programmer go about coding it? As with simple branching there is a multitude of possibilities, but here we can apply some criteria to select the best way. My personal criteria are as follows:

(a) It must be reasonably efficient.

(b) The end of the loop must be clearly demarcated. The best language in this respect is probably BASIC, with its excellent

```
10   FOR I = 1 TO N
50   NEXT I
```

(c) It must use a leading test, so that the equivalent of

```
10 FOR I = 1 to 0
50 NEXT I
```

never gets executed.

Two structures which satisfy both (a) and (c) are

```
        LOOP1 N;CT
        ----------
[1]         CT←0
[2]       L:→(N<CT←CT+1)↑EXIT
[3]         'PROCESS ',▼CT
[4]            →L
[5]    EXIT:'READY'
         ∇
```

and

```
        LOOP2 N;CT;LAB
        --------------
[1]          →LAB←(NρL),EXIT,CT←1
[2]        L:'PROCESS ',▼CT
[3]          →LAB[CT←CT+1]
[4]     EXIT:'READY'
         ∇
```

I prefer the second version for two main reasons: it makes it clear that the end of the loop is not an ordinary branch, thus satisfying (b), and it is about 20% faster for loops of more than 20 or so iterations (see Table 4.2).

Table 4.2   Relative timings of LOOP1 and LOOP2

No. of iterations	LOOP1 (ms)	LOOP2 (ms)
10	4	6
50	15	13
100	30	25
1000	283	239

Often it is not even necessary to set up a counter; for example to process a work variable VEC an element at a time you could use

```
        VEC←0,VEC
LP:→(ρVEC←1↓VEC)↓DONE
    ⍴PROCESS VEC[1]
        →LP
DONE:'READY'
```

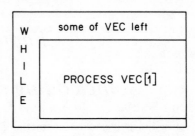

If you ever find yourself writing a nested loop in APL, I strongly suggest you try to find another way of doing it. Either that or your next time-sharing bill is going to be a bit of a shock!

I could happily ramble on through APL style for many pages more, but unfortunately style isn't the only ingredient of successful APL; discipline is essential too, and it is to that subject that I turn next. However, the theme of style and structure does recur in Chapter 10, which includes several more examples of the block diagrams I have introduced here.

Chapter 5

Some coding conventions

Just for once I'm going to be dogmatic. The benefits to be gained from a bit of coding standardization are so great that the tiny amount of effort needed to follow a few simple rules is repaid many times over. Whether you are an APL loner or a member of a vast development team this means you. Why standardize? Here are a few good reasons:

(a) APL lays many traps for the unwary, some of them quite subtle ones. A few simple conventions and you will never stray near them.

(b) Someone else (or yourself in a few years' time) may actually be able to understand your programs. This could save a lot of good work from the scrap-heap.

(c) You'll be safe from disaster when the system changes around you, or if you come in-house from a bureau.

If you've been writing APL for a while, you must by now have your own view of what constitutes good coding practice. I hope you will read the rest of this for interest, but I would happily concede that your conventions are just as valid as mine. If you are quite new to APL, then I suggest that you follow the rules I give, at least to start with. Sooner or later you will inevitably need to break most of them, but at least by then you will know why you are breaking them, and you'll be well aware of the pitfalls they are designed to keep you away from.

I want to start with naming conventions, because it is in the potential confusion of APL objects that the worst of the hazards lie.

- *Rule 1.* Always use mnemonic names for functions and variables.

Function names tend to derive from verbs, variable names from nouns. Where a sub-function is essentially 'local' to its calling function (i.e. it is not called from anywhere else, nor is it likely to be), preface its name with one or two characters from the name of the calling function. For example EDIT may call EDΔDISPLAY and EDΔUPDATE, and by naming them thus you ensure that they are listed together by your documentation programs. Standard system utilities get 'Δ' as a preface, and should normally be locked, to ensure they don't get listed.

- *Rule 2.* Names of global variables should be prefaced with 'Δ'. This identifies them clearly, and makes the job of tracking down any stray variables which should have been localized that much easier. Of course the corollary is that names of local variables should not include characters other than 'A–Z' and '1–9'.

- *Rule 3*. Labels should again be mnemonics, and should have the first letter underlined. Label variables should be underlined in their entirety, e.g.

```
→LAB←((ρVAR)ρLOOP),EXIT
```

Of course LAB must be explicitly localized in the function header. Pedants note I have just broken Rule 2 as LAB is really just another local variable!

Incidentally I have frequently come across recommended labelling schemes – such as 'L1, L2, . . . , etc.' or 'A, B, C, . . . , etc.' – in which the labels increment in some way as you move down the function. For languages like COBOL and FORTRAN this clearly makes sense, because in a program which runs to many pages it is vital to know roughly where a branch is going to. In APL (see Rule 7) it should always be possible to view an entire function at a glance, so the L1, L2, . . . convention adds nothing to the clarity of the listing.

These three rules should steer you well clear of any potential name conflicts. As an example of the potential confusion that can arise when names clash, consider the following:

```
    UPDATE;ROW
    ----------

[1]         ⍝CHANGE/DELETE TABLE ENTRIES
                  .
                  .
[15] DELETE:UPD∆DEL ROW
                  .
                  .



    DELETE
    ------

[1]    ⍝REMOVE LAST WEEKS FIGURES
              .
              .
```

Just suppose that UPDATE gets suspended for some reason; then if the user types in 'DELETE' he will get the unlikely response '15' and not a lot else! On a terminal or VDU without an APL keyboard this is not just embarrassing – it is a serious problem, and one which could so easily have been avoided. If you follow Rules 1–3 you leave open one potential conflict only: that between local variables and top-level functions. However, variable names tend to be noun-based and function names are derived from verbs, so this apparent flaw in the system is unlikely ever to trouble you. I for one, would far rather live with it than resort to 'WK1, WK2, . . . ' or some such for my local names.

That covers naming conventions. Now for something rather more controversial!

- *Rule 4.* Never use zero-origin, either globally or locally. The gain in elegance is minimal and the cost in future confusion considerable.

Lovers of zero-origin should admit that they form a shrinking minority, and that their programs will one day be changed by someone who has never strayed from the safe ground of one-origin. They should also realize what a pest they are to anyone responsible for system utilities; zero-origin may be fun, but origin-independence most certainly is not!

The next couple of rules deal with the way functions link together.

- *Rule 5.* Where possible, values should be passed in to functions as arguments, not allowed to float across in global variables.

I can think of two exceptions to this one:

(a) Where many arguments of different data types must be passed. Clearly the APL syntax allows for no more than two, and the process of stringing them all together outside the called function, then digging them out again inside, is highly tedious.

(b) Where storage is at a premium. It will definitely pay not to double up the storage taken by large objects, which is what some APL interpreters do when parameters are passed.

If you are forced into using floating variables, please document the fact clearly in both the called and calling functions.

- *Rule 6.* Functions (except possibly right at the top level) should always return specific results.

This applies particularly to utility functions which are to go on general release; it is not at all obvious to the author just how his creation might get incorporated into someone else's system. A classic example of how not to do it is in the IBM distributed workspace PLOT. Suppose you have a routine called ΔPR which prints character matrices on the line printer; you might think that you could type

```
[1]     ΔPR 'HERE IS A GRAPH'
[2]     ΔPR 20 60 PLOT ΔDATA
```

- no chance! Because PLOT simply displays its output rather than returning it, all line 2 will achieve is a VALUE ERROR!

In many ways arguments and results are like the knobs and sockets on the pieces of a jigsaw puzzle; without them there is no way of linking the pieces together.

So far I have dealt mainly with ways and means of making your life easier during system development. If the system is definitely a one-off, or if it is purely for your own use, Rules 1–6 are probably enough to see you through. The rules that follow are designed to make life easier for those who come after you.

I have frequently seen the argument that APL programs are virtually unmaintainable, even by the system author. It seems to me that the opposite is true; with good structuring and proper documentation an APL system can be maintained and modified far more easily than a program written in, say, FORTRAN. The key concept is that of 'disposable code'; you should no more think of re-working an APL function than you would of attempting to repair an IC on a circuit board. If it doesn't work, throw it away and get a new one. The philosophy of modular replacement is simple enough; to apply it in an APL system is quite straightforward, but again there are one or two conventions to follow.

- *Rule 7.* No function should be longer than one page, or about 40 statements.

In a VDU system functions that fit on one screen are obviously preferable, but in practice a limit of 20 statements seems too restrictive. It merely encourages fanatics to cram yet more code on to each line!

Three oft-encountered exceptions are as follows:

(a) Functions such as 'DESCRIBE' or 'HELP'.

(b) Reporting functions where quite complex printer layouts must be set up.

(c) System utilities such as workspace documentation or full-screen panel design. These are rather a special case, as they will be erased from the workspace before the system goes live.

Leaving these aside, it would be hard to over-emphasize the benefits of breaking a system down into manageable modules. It will be easier to code, easier to test, and feasible to maintain.

- *Rule 8.* It should be possible to re-create any function from the comments alone.

Of course APL is so rich in constructs that the new function may have very little resemblance to its predecessor; the point is that it will do exactly the same job when viewed from outside. This is more than just the usual plea to programmers to document their work; APL *is* hard to decipher and anyone who fails to comment adequately is placing a terrible burden on the shoulders of all who follow. Probably the two most important factors in favour of APL are the speed with which systems can be put together, and the ease with which they can be changed. To sacrifice the second of these in exchange for insignificant gains in the first really is the height of folly. Moral: write the comments first, then fill in the code.

- *Rule 9.* Each function should do one clearly defined task.

Functions which switch between several tasks depending on passed parameters are laying up trouble for the future. At this level, keep the structure almost childishly simple; coding *tours de force* should be safely tucked away in the lowest-level functions where they need never be seen again.

Before I close this chapter, there are a few minor points which are basically common-sense, but probably ought to be said:

- Never branch to line numbers, or to □LC + n.

- Use a standard branching method. I suggest take and drop (see Chapter 4) for if/if not.

- Don't overdo the one-liner. In particular never use '. . . , 0ρ . . . ', and beware of multiple assignments on the same line.

- Try to give each function a single exit point, i.e. use →EXIT, not →0.

- Only lock functions when it's absolutely necessary. Before locking them clear out all comments and labels with a suitable utility. Be very careful not to lose the unlocked copy, for example by overwriting it with the locked version.

- If you copy and change a system utility, always re-name it.

- Never use □AV explicitly. Sooner or later it will change under you; so put things like terminal control characters and graphics into ΔTC,ΔGR, etc., and index these. It won't cost you anything, and it could save an awful lot of bother.

- Bury things like file access and full-screen management in utility functions. Again this could save a great deal of trouble if you have to move your APL systems to a new environment.

- Retract and expunge shared variables as soon as you have finished with them.

- Always put something into □LX, even if only a one-line description of the workspace.

I think that just about covers it. As I said at the start of this chapter, the main thing is to find any workable set of conventions and to stick to it. By doing this you will get systems off the ground faster, and you will pave the way for the evolutionary approach to design outlined in Chapter 2. You will also find yourself with systems that are virtually self-documenting and that can be easily and quickly changed in the future. If I had to pick out two key elements in the conventions I have given, I would choose (a) breaking the application down into its functional units and (b) avoiding 'floating' variables. The first of these is essential both during development and for the future; the value of the second only really becomes apparent when a long-standing system is changed.

In these last two chapters the emphasis has been on writing APL code. I now want to move back to the main thread of the book, which is writing APL systems, although I admit that the two strands can never be wholly separated. That, after all, is one of the things that makes APL different.

Chapter 6

A new methodology

In this chapter I want to draw some threads together. I want to show how the evolutionary philosophy of Chapter 2, the structure and style of Chapter 4, and the coding conventions of Chapter 5 can be combined into a new methodology. I suspect that many of my readers have come to APL and APL systems with no prior knowledge of computing, and that they must be wondering what all the fuss is about. After all, how else do you write systems in APL?! This chapter is really aimed at those who have spent their careers in DP departments, perhaps first as programmers and then as analysts: people who, like myself, find their thinking conditioned by years of conventional systems development. It is not easy to change one's whole attitude to life, but change we must, otherwise the revolution will pass us by.

As with all revolutions, this one has had the unfortunate effect of polarizing attitudes. With DP fighting off what it sees as an attack on its traditional patch, and the bureaux scrambling for lucrative new business, there is ample scope for strong words. The bureaux' view is one of users retiring baffled at talk of 'resource conflicts' and 'man years', only to find that an APL terminal fulfils their needs in days. On the other hand, there must be many, many cases of inexperienced users getting into a frightful (and expensive) tangle with badly thought out, poorly designed systems; in fact making all the mistakes that the DP industry made 20 years ago! Today you can get a decent APL microcomputer for well under £20 000, so here is yet a third element to add to the already confused scene! One thing is certain – if APL is to fulfil its true potential as a systems-building tool, we must find a way of bringing these diverse elements together.

In DP we must stop imagining that we can go on muttering 'project evaluation' or 'unprofessional approach', and generally behaving like a dinosaur which has just had its tail hacked off. The bureaux, on the other hand, should stop over-selling APL, without also providing the knowledge and experience to use it wisely. This chapter sets out to describe an approach to building APL systems which I hope will help anyone with an APL terminal on his desk. Whether it is to a bureau, an APL micro, or a mainframe computer, then this method should get you results in the sort of time you expected when you originally hired the terminal. If you work in a DP department, perhaps as a systems analyst, then I hope I can persuade you that there is a systems methodology for APL, and that maybe the APL approach is not so unprofessional after all – just different.

Back to the start: you are a middle-manager with a terminal on your desk, or a programmer-analyst who has just had a request for help. Your ultimate aim is to

44

weld a successful team from the user and the computer, with yourself a discreet distance away. In fact you are trying to get from

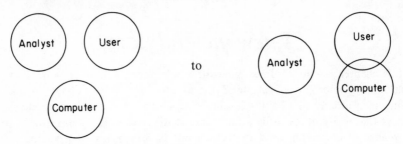

to

How should you proceed? Well, Stage 1 is easy enough, particularly if you are programming your own system!

Stage 1 – Get to Know the People

The social context of a system really does matter. Not just who is to use the system, but who they work for and what the local politics are. Who are the people with a vested interest in the success of the system? How can you work round those who would like to maintain the *status quo*? What incentives can you offer to those who don't care either way? Don't expect to get it all right straight away – you don't have to. It's easy enough to plot a course through departmental politics as long as you keep enough options open, and remain willing to adapt to a change in climate. In terms of the relationships sketched above, what you have now achieved is

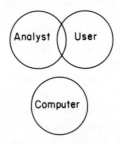

Stage 2 – Get Them Used to the Computer

Most people's experience of computers is limited to bits of paper that arrive through the post every so often – mainly bills or the occasional unwanted circular. Is it any wonder that they will view the entry of the machine into their own little world with something less than delight? It is up to the analyst to overcome this aversion, because overcome it he must, and soon. He needs more than just passive acceptance of the system; without the active involvement of the user from the very early stages all his work may count for nothing. Fortunately we have in APL the ideal vehicle for the 'acclimatization' process; it is the work of but a few days to knock together a little workspace of demonstration functions. Then you can invite your clients to a bit of 'hands on' computing; start from '2+2', let them beat it at noughts and crosses a few times, and generally get across to them the impression that the computer is fun. A trip round the computer room is no bad idea either – all the flashing lights and humming disk drives are impressive in their own right, but equally important is the impression of people being in control. In all my experience of taking groups of users round our machine room the thing that seemed to fascinate people most was the operator's console! Incidentally it's well worth leaving a few games programs kicking around in the system, they may get misused occasionally but they are the best advertising gimmick ever invented!

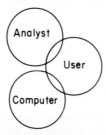

is the result of this stage.

Stage 3 – Pin Down Some Data

The hardest part of any new application is getting started; you can't evolve a system from nothing. If you can dig out some elements from the mess which are liable to stay reasonably constant, then deal with these first. Very often this means data of one form or another; planning systems, for example, tend to feed on tables of machine-rates, or on sales estimates which arrive from elsewhere. Work done programming these is unlikely to need re-doing and will give the rest of the system some firm anchorages. It will also do wonders for your credibility, and this will be a big help later.

You can also try to spot the most likely utility functions which you may want later. If these exist, copy them from a public library, otherwise get them written now. The evolution of the final system will be a much smoother process if most of the building material is readily to hand.

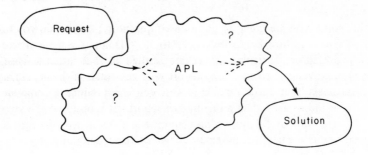

has become

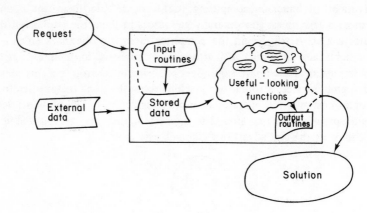

Stage 4 – Programming by Negotiation

This, of course, is the crux of the matter. You, the analyst, now know a bit about the user's problems, and quite a lot about the kind of programs you can build for him. Defining the data has done that much for you. From the other side of the relationship, the user has had to think in more depth than usual about what he wants, and is beginning to appreciate the sort of things an APL system can do.

The relationship between user, analyst and computer is at its most tightly knit, and now looks like

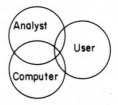

There is just enough of an overlap to get a constructive dialogue going, and an initial system will soon emerge. If you have guessed right about the utilities, and have set up the basic data sensibly, it should be easy enough to assemble this. In fact a lot of the programming can probably be done with the user sitting beside you at the terminal. This is where you really start reaping the benefits of that modular approach!

At this point, you are going to get a lot of questions like '... do you think we could ... ?' or '... how easy would it be to ... ?' Don't take these at face value! Find out why those particular figures are wanted in that rather strange order. Suggest alternatives – often in a long report with sub-totals all he is actually after is the total lines! You know that with APL you can produce a complete cross-tabulation far more easily than a line-by-line report – it is up to you to say so. The result will be a more useful system programmed in a fraction of the time it would have taken had all the user's requirements been interpreted literally.

I suppose the hardest part is to avoid the 'You would like it like this, wouldn't you?' approach. If a user has a very clear idea of exactly what he wants, then by all means question him closely on 'why?', but be prepared to write the system basically as he wants it. At the opposite extreme is the user who will instinctively recognize the right approach when you eventually find it, but who won't have the first idea how to set about describing it to you in the abstract. Here there is a very considerable danger of putting words into his mouth! Be patient - keep fishing for information, keep putting bits of code together, keep checking how he reacts. You'll get there in the end, by which time you'll probably understand his job as well as he does!

As with all successful collaborations, this one is based on mutual respect: you must respect the user's experience and ability to do his job; you must gain his respect by proving your ability to get results from the computer. I used the word 'symbiosis' in Chapter 2 to express the way an interactive computing system should spring from the fusion of the user's know-how and the computer's power; it is largely up to you to create the conditions in which this can occur.

Stage 5 - Refining the Dialogue

What you should have by now is a reasonably firm database, a group of fairly robust functions to maintain it, and a motley assortment of rather fragile code which feeds on it. If you are both programmer and user, then you can cheerfully skip this stage - what does it matter if the dialogue is a trifle illogical, and might collapse if you hit 'enter' at the wrong moment? You are, after all, always going to be on hand to straighten things out! If, on the other hand, you are developing a system for someone else to use, then you may be over the hump intellectually, but you still have a lot of programming to do!

I think the hallmark of a good dialogue is probably its invisibility - like a well trained butler in a Victorian household it should do its job unobtrusively, but should always be on hand if its master needs help. This is the ideal; how the APL programmer sets about achieving it is another matter! For one thing, the nature of the dialogue will depend enormously on the type of terminal being used; when a system is transferred from a teletype to a VDU environment what was previously compact and efficient becomes terribly long-winded and slow. That said, I shall now try first to make some general points about dialogue design, then to mention one or two specific to teletype-driven systems, and finally to discuss the very different approach which a VDU environment permits.

First, then, dialogues in general and some fairly sweeping statements to which I'm sure you can find exceptions:

- The application must be totally robust. No conceivable combination of unlikely actions by the user should give an APL error message. If you have error-trapping, use it with care as a final long-stop, not as your standard catch-all.

- Keep the system 'open' (see Chapter 4) unless there is a good reason to do otherwise. If, by closing part of the system, you can make it more efficient without in any way losing flexibility, then do so. Otherwise beware of being over-protective! Users are at least as intelligent and inventive as you are; as long as you tell them the rules then it is perfectly safe to let them loose into the system. As new situations arise, the user will often be able to cope with them without requiring a formal change in the dialogue. This removes the burden of designing a system which is itself adaptive. To quote from a paper in the 1979 UK Operational Research Conference (Tobin, 1980):

> 'If a model is highly interactive it is also highly flexible and the necessary adaptation can take place in the man, who can be more sensitive to the changing constraints and objectives. After the man has adapted, it will very likely be found expedient to adapt the model.'

In my view, a totally closed system is a very effective way of preventing such adaptation!

- Like it or not you are designing a language, and you must make it consistent. If you ask for dates in 'DD/MM/YY' format, then always display them like this. Use a consistent command (e.g. 'STOP', or just 'carriage return') to escape from input routines. If you have six different reports, print 'REPORT 1', 'REPORT 2', etc., on the top of each. It is little things like this that provide the positive feedback to the user, and confirm that he does know where he is in the system.

What then of teletype dialogues? The overwhelming constraint here must be the speed (or otherwise!) of the terminal, so every effort must be made to cut down the system's verbosity:

- Keep wordy input prompts for 'first-time' users. Switch to short messages as soon as possible.

- Make it possible to stack up the answers to a series of questions when answering the first. For example to enter data to a personnel system one might see

```
NAME:  Fred Bloggs
AGE:   24
DEPT:  Op. Res.
NAME:  Joe Soap
etc.
```

or

```
NAME:  Fred Bloggs, 24, Op. Res.
NAME:  Joe Soap, . . .
etc.
```

For one way of doing this, see STACK in Chapter 8.

- If you use menu-selection, don't re-display the menu every time. Users are perfectly capable of remembering that 'REPORT' is option 5; you can always give them a reference card for complex parts of the system.

- Only print lengthy descriptive information under extreme provocation, or if the user specifically requests it.

- In a complex tree of menus, it should be possible to escape from the lowest level right back to the top without going through all the intermediate prompts.

Finally, what about APL systems for VDUs? Until recently APL handled the screen rather like an overgrown teletype, using only the bottom line for input, and the remainder for output. In this environment one could relax many of the above restrictions, e.g. menus could be displayed every time, but the fundamental structure of the dialogue was unchanged. No more than one line of data could ever be entered at a time (without stacking anyway); there was certainly room only for a single input prompt. Now all that has changed: full-screen management is upon us, and suddenly we are all playing to very different rules.

As an example of just how different the full-screen approach is, I want to quote some dialogue from a system which I wrote for a teletype, and have since rewritten for VDU. Twelve components were manufactured on a three-shift system during the week; the system time-tabled the production of these around an assortment of constraints, such as stock levels and available labour. However, it was necessary for the planner to be able to stop the system time-tabling certain components on certain days on an *ad hoc* basis. The dialogue went something like this:

```
BAN                              (the name of the function)
COMPONENT: WIDGET
WHICH DAY, SHIFT: MON PM
COMPONENT: SPROCKET, WED AM      (notice the stack)
etc.
```

The functions to achieve all this took (excluding the STACK utility) around 40 statements, and had to make provision for invalid component names and unrecognized DAY/SHIFT abbreviations. The end result was to update a 12 by 21 matrix, assigning zeros into the banned slots, and ones elsewhere. Using full-screen management, the entire dialogue becomes totally unnecessary! All we have to do is display the matrix on the screen, using 'X' to represent slots already banned, hold it there while the planner types 'X' in the appropriate positions, read it back, and re-assign into the matrix. Not only does this take the user half the time (about one-fifth of the CPU time incidentally) but it effectively removes any possible sources of error. The result is a far more elegant and comprehensible piece of program, taking eight statements instead of 40-odd! Obviously I want to take a more detailed look at full-screen management, and Chapter 9 reviews this topic in depth.

That covers most of what I want to say on dialogue design in APL. I still believe that producing a good dialogue is more of an art than a science, and that the title of Stage 4 – 'Programming by negotiation' – remains a good description of the way

50

a dialogue develops. You may find bits of any dialogue irritatingly slow or imprecise, but if your user is happy, then let it be. On the other hand there may be parts of the dialogue which you find perfectly clear and concise, but which regularly confuse the user! These are the areas to tinker with; remember that original criterion of invisibility!

Before I leave this section on dialogue I would like to throw in one or two mildly heretical thoughts on validation. In the traditional batch system data is keyed to cards or disk by a punch operator who has no way of recognizing a daft figure. The data is then processed, maybe overnight, and any errors get reported the day after. Of course if any error actually crashes one of the programs the DP department might be in serious trouble, with its schedules thrown out at least for that night. Otherwise the corrected data will go back into the system for a final run the day after. Because data errors can slip so easily into the system, and because of the damage they may cause, the writer of a big batch system must pay great attention to his validation routines. For people like myself who have grown up in this batch world, it is very difficult to adjust psychologically to the different needs of APL.

To take the simplest case first: a program for your own use where you are always going to be the one who enters the figures. It's doubtful if you even need a numeric check, so why not just use quad input? It probably is worth doing a length check on vectors though, even if only

```
MAT←MAT,[1] (1↓ρMAT)↑,⎕
```

This saves the embarrassment of LENGTH ERRORS and you often want to pad to the right with zeros anyway. It's also worth re-displaying the data at some point; the sort of errors you are likely to make (like missing a figure out) will show up clearly enough.

Most APL systems fall into a category midway between this case and the batch approach. They are used by someone other than the author, but the user is directly responsible for the entry of data. This has two important consequences: the user will take considerable pains to get the figures right, and he will spot a mistake straight away. This really reduces the programmer's task to the simple one of making sure that if a thumb-fingered user hits a few wrong keys then nothing actually stops. A simple re-display of the entered figures before filing them is always a good idea, but is probably only practical on a VDU-based system.

One final point on VDU-based data–editing. The keys to worry about are things like 'CLEAR' and 'ERASE INPUT' which can do far stranger things to a full-screen editor than any combination of wrong numbers!

Stage 6 – Digging Yourself Out

Sooner or later there comes a point where the system must be allowed to make its own way in the world without constant guidance from its programmer. Even in systems which are entirely for your personal use, you can't really afford to go crawling into the code every time something isn't quite to your liking. In a production system stability is vital to the user's confidence, and you should never change anything without first making sure that *all* the interested parties have been consulted, and know exactly what is going to change, and when.

In terms of my 'ACU' cartoon, we must take the final step of disengaging the analyst from the rest:

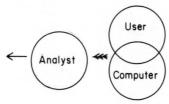

Two of the best ways of achieving this stability are documentation and education. A properly documented system can be put away for long periods, and yet still be maintained at a moment's notice, either by the author or by any other competent APL programmer. This removes the need for the author to remain constantly in touch (and hence the temptation constantly to tinker!) with the innards of the system. The role of user-education in achieving stability stems mainly from the considerable investment of time and energy the author must make whenever a new education program is needed. In a stable system 'local experts' soon develop among the regular users, and the job of training people new to the application will quickly be taken off the analyst's hands.

To summarize the progression through Stages 1-6:

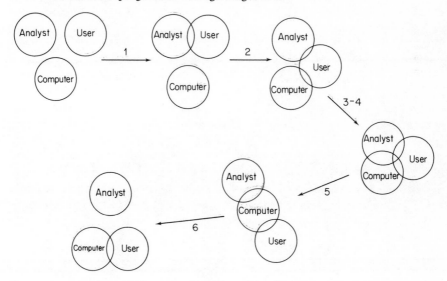

. . . which makes it all look deceptively straightforward! In practice of course, different bits of the system will be at different stages, and you may often find yourself backtracking to attack areas which somehow got left out first time through. As for documentation, that obviously merits a chapter to itself, so I think that just about wraps up this ramble through the APL methodology. Yes, it is different, it is unstructured, it is unpredictable, but it gets the job done and that, in the end, is what counts.

Chapter 7

Documenting an APL system

There are two types of APL system, two types of documentation, and two places where it may be kept:

- *Personal systems* are systems put together entirely for the author's own use;

- *Production systems* are systems written for others to use, and on which some significant part of a company's operation depends.

- *System documentation* explains how the system works;

- *User documentation* explains how the system is to be used.

- *Internal documentation* is held in the workspace(s) that make up the system;

- *External documentation* is held on paper in a manual/project file, etc.

When documenting an APL sytem, you must first decide which type it is: personal or production. (If the former, is it certain to remain so?) Then apply the criteria below to be sure that your level of documentation is at least adequate.

Personal systems

	Internal	External
System	Reasonably modular Sufficiently commented Follows a naming convention	? function listings ? Relationships between variables

User	Brief "DESCRIBE" as $\Box LX$
	Helpful prompts
		Included on a list of all
		  your systems with a
		  brief note of what it
		  does

Virtually all the documentation is internal, making it:

- easily updated
- readily available
- inseparable from the system

Thus you have no excuse for omitting to change the documentation as (or before) you change the code. You will always be able to refer to it when you most need to, and you won't risk losing the one scrap of paper which just happened to have these vital notes on it!

For personal systems, the prime purpose of the system documentation must be to make change as easy as possible. Comments need be little more than brief notes to yourself, but they should still be there. Things which are obvious when a function is written may be anything but in two years' time; for one thing your style may have changed markedly by then. The value of modular code, and of strict adherence to a naming convention, I hope I made clear in Chapter 5. You may not need any external system documentation at all, but if you have access to some suitable utilities, then a set of function listings won't come amiss. The other thing I often find rather handy is a rough diagram showing the relationships between the various APL variables in the workspace. I think I can best explain what I mean with an example: suppose we have a little APL system to keep a log of our company's foreign exchange commitments. This will have variables such as

ΔAMOUNT	vector of outstanding quantitites
ΔDATE	date each is due
ΔDESCR	matrix of descriptions of each
ΔCCY	index into currency table
ΔCREF	matrix of currency names
ΔRATES	exchange rates (spot and forward) for each currency

I would draw these as follows:

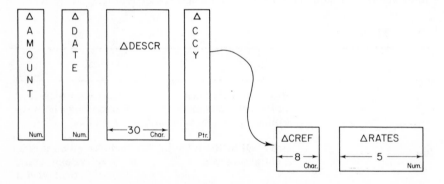

clearly depicting the relationships among the various data entities. This sort of chart makes clear where the potential traps lie. For example:

- To delete an entry from the log we must apply the same mask to ΔAMOUNT, ΔDATE, ΔDESCR, and ΔCCY, but *not* to ΔCREF or ΔRATES.

- To delete a currency from the system, we must delete any log entries for that currency and we must also adjust the remaining elements of ΔCCY, which would otherwise point to the wrong place.

The use of such data structures will crop up again in Chapter 12, in the section on efficient use of storage.

The internal user documentation is again no more than a few reminders; a very abbreviated DESCRIBE won't take long to type in, and will save the occasional browse through)FNS when you forget what your top-level functions are called. I doubt if you need any external user documentation at all. Perhaps just a note of the workspace name and a one-line abstract of what it does.

Production systems

	Internal	External

System	Highly modular
	All functions re-creatable
	  from the comments alone
	Strict use of naming
	  conventions
	Very straightforward code
		Function listings
		Function cross-reference
		Function tree-structure
		Variable-function
		  cross-reference
		Chart of variable
		  relationships
		Screen-panel listings
		Workspace summary
		Function specifications
		Summary of file access

User	'DESCRIBE' pointing to
	  more detailed 'HOWXXX'
	  functions
	Long/short prompts
	  (teletype)
	HELP frames (full-screen)
	'AUTHOR' giving name
	  and phone number of
	  contact
	'RELEASE' giving current
	  release number and date
		Some notes on the
		  hardware, e.g. siting of
		  VDUs, keyboard train-
		  ing, log-on, etc.
		What to do when some-
		  thing goes wrong
		System user-guide:
		  notes on all the com-
		  mands; the general
		  style of dialogue, and
		  specific prompts
		  which might cause
		  trouble
		A clear description of
		  the library commands,
		  i.e.)LOAD, etc.
		A clear statement of any
		  known limitations,
		  e.g. quantity of data

Before I go on to take each of the four areas in more detail, I want to tackle the general point of how big an application can be before it should be split over several workspaces. The penalty of splitting a system up in this way is the introduction of an additional level of external documentation over and above that needed for each workspace. For example

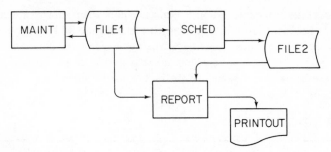

where workspace 'MAINT' contains the functions to read and update data on machine speeds, etc. (held on FILE1); 'SCHED' uses this data to produce a production time-table, which it stores on FILE2; 'REPORT' uses the data on machine speeds again to print the stored schedule.

Such system flowcharts can get surprisingly complicated alarmingly quickly, and you will also need some sort of summary of contents and access for all the files. However, splitting an application up in this way does keep the contents of each workspace within reasonable limits. Again it's a personal view, but I feel that an application should be split up when it totals around 2000 lines of APL (i.e. 80-100 functions), and that once split each section should be kept below about 1000 lines from then on. An advantage of this fragmentation is, slightly paradoxically, a more 'user-friendly' system. Most users are much happier with three or four workspaces each with, say seven commands, than with one workspace having over 20 commands.

Enough, anyway, of this digression. What about the documentation needed for each workspace, and, from the user's point of view, for the system as a whole? Stick rigorously to the coding conventions of Chapter 5 (i.e. follow a strict naming convention, write the comments first, avoid floating variables like the plague, keep functions short) and you can't go far wrong. There are only two further suggestions I would make: have a function (or variable) 'HOWGLOBALS' which describes in detail the contents, nature, and purpose of all your global variables; secondly, if you do any file access, then a similar function 'HOWFILES' should list all the files read/written/updated, with details of the variables fetched from/dumped to each file.

What then of the external system documentation (otherwise known as paperwork, bumf, etc.)? – the completion of which always seems to form Stage 5 of the well-trained analyst's progress to fame and fortune!

Let's start with a nice fat folder, with the workspace name clearly written on the spine, and decide what ought to go into it. Obviously a complete set of function listings, a cross-reference of function calls, and a cross-reference of global-function references. All this can easily be produced automatically (see Chapter 10) as can a pictorial representation of any full-screen panels, and a separate listing of any 'HOW' or 'DESCRIBE' functions. So far, so good, and the additional paperwork needed is pretty minimal. I would suggest using forms along the lines of Figures 7.1-7.3: the first as a checklist; the second as a paper back-up for the 'DESCRIBE' and 'HOW-FILES' functions; the third to fill any gaps left by your program comments. In

Workspace Name _____

	Contents		Initials
1	System Flowchart		
2	Workspace Specification		
3	File Layouts		
4	Function Specifications		
5	Global Variable Descriptions		
6	WS Structure Analysis (Tree Diagram)	Document Utility	
7	Function Listings		
8	Function Cross - reference		
9	Global Variable Cross-reference		
10	VDU Layouts		
11	Printer Layouts		
12			

Figure 7.1   APL workspace run book contents

particular this 'function specification' makes specific provision for those quasi-globals which can cause so much trouble, and it gives space for a reasonably full description of the arguments and results. In my experience these are the quantities most likely to be of interest to the future APL programmers who must amend (or debug) your system. Whether you need a typed 'global variable' description depends on whether or not you already have 'HOWGLOBALS' in the workspace, which leaves only item 11 on Figure 7.1 - the printer layouts. These I find something of a bugbear, because I normally draft them rather roughly and then mess around with the code until the report looks right. I think the best compromise is probably an annotated sample of output, with notes on the field widths, starting columns, etc., where these are likely to be relevant in the future.

For the great majority of APL systems this really is all you need - after years spent 'completing the documentation' of conventional systems the APL philosophy

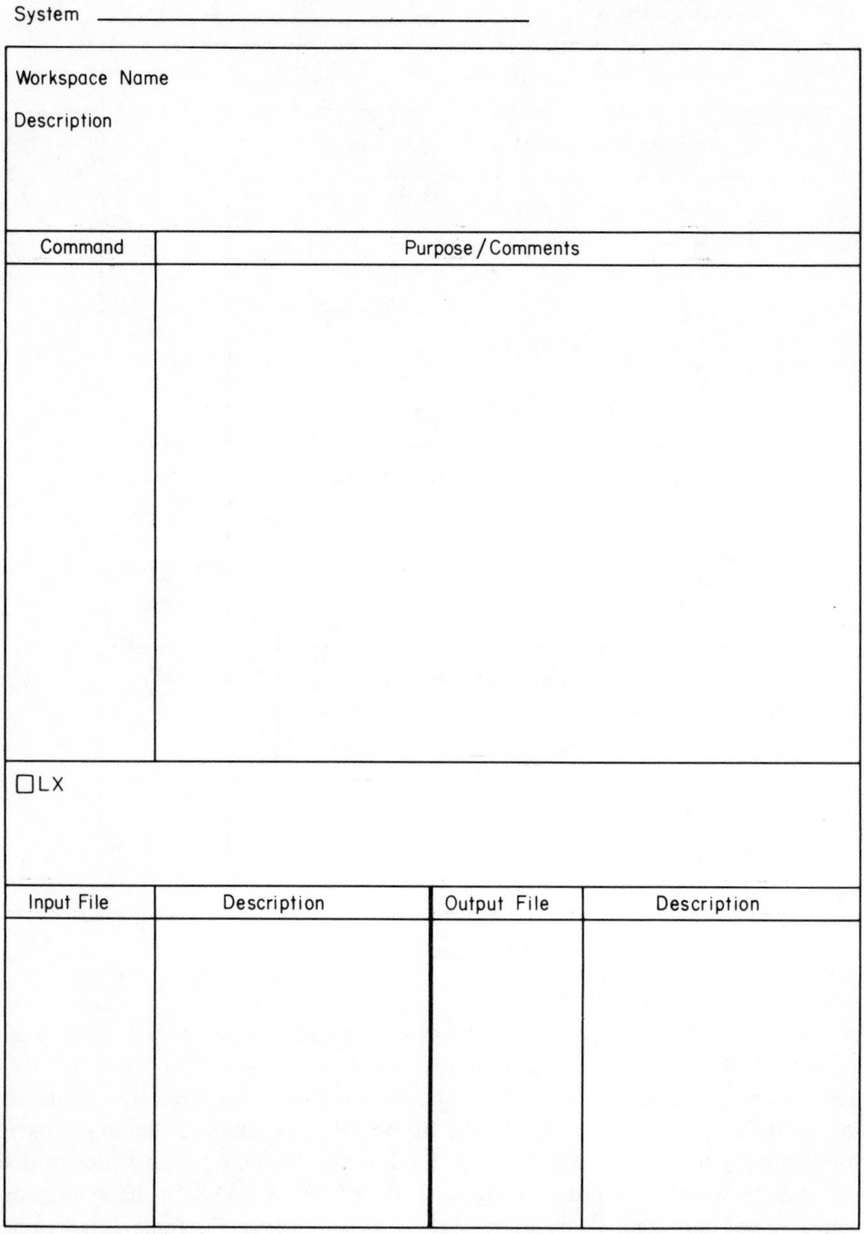

58

System _____

Workspace Name	
Description	
Command	Purpose / Comments
☐LX	
Input File	Description	Output File	Description

Figure 7.2   APL workspace specification

comes as a blessed relief to the over-worked analyst or programmer! Why is there
so much less paperwork? Well, one obvious reason is the way APL cuts down the
lines of communication which separate the user from the system. Every link in the

System _____

Function			
Argument (s)			
Returning			

Purpose

Description

Common Vars Set Up	C/N	Shape	Description

Common Vars Referenced	Localized in Function		

Figure 7.3   APL function specification

chain meant a form to fill in, and even a simple program amendment could generate an absurd amount of waste paper.

Finally, on the subject of paper documentation, I want to offer a few thoughts on the rather vexed question of 'documenting the algorithm'. What on Earth do we do when a brilliant young OR man, after months of apparently unproductive head-scratching, suddenly invents an inspired way of solving some planning problem? Uttering strange cries he makes a bee-line for the nearest APL terminal, there to remain until his brainchild has taken shape. Even as he adds the finishing touches he places his manager firmly on the horns of a particularly unpleasant dilemma! Such solutions are the work of one man alone; how can the department possibly offer credible back-up and maintenance when that man leaves? My view is that APL was conceived for just this purpose! We shouldn't lose sight of the fact that it is first and foremost a means of expressing complex algorithms clearly and concisely, *not* a means of programming computers. If, by providing them with an APL interpreter, the OR department forces its bright boys to write their algorithms in a consistent and powerful notation, then I would argue that it has taken a big step along the road to maintainability. With an APL system, paper documentation of algorithms is essentially unnecessary!

Back to firmer ground with the next item on the list – internal user documentation. Again let me start with a plea for open systems. In a closed system every choice means a menu, and every menu needs a 'HELP' function. In particular it is all too easy to get a user lost somewhere near the top of a tree, when he really wanted to be on a different branch altogether. The best user documentation in the world won't get him out of this one! In an open system the user is never more than one command away from APL, and thus never more than two commands away from 'DESCRIBE'. Because there are no complex trees to get lost in, the total amount of 'HELP' in the workspace is minimal, and can be kept to specifics, such as the correct format for dates, or the known abbreviations for the machines in a production scheduling system. Two other functions which I might leave lying around are 'AUTHOR' and 'RELEASE'. The former simply gives the users a phone number to ring in case of trouble; the latter returns a release number (and date) and would normally be included in the Latent Execution. This is particularly useful where many copies of a workspace are in existence, and you do not necessarily know that all your users have furnished themselves with the most recent one. If someone rings up with a problem it is very convenient to be able to ask them to type 'RELEASE', so that you know straight away which version of the program you are dealing with.

So far all this documention requires some specific action on the user's part to get at it. Equally important is the documentation he gets willy-nilly as part of the dialogue. At this point there is again a marked divergence between teletype and VDU systems; the former being much the simpler of the two to deal with, but the latter far more satisfactory when you get it right. As always, what the teletype system must fight is the speed of the terminal. How to provide enough information for the novice user, and yet not slow the system down so that it infuriates the expert? There are two basic ways of attacking the problem: the use of alternative long/short prompts; and the provision of stacking, so that the expert can bypass most of the prompts altogether. Which method you use (of course there's no reason why you shouldn't use both!) is largely a matter of personal preference. Another way out, and one which I have used perfectly successfully, is to stick to brief prompts throughout and to compile a comprehensive user-guide which gives the more detailed explanations.

The problems in producing a 'friendly' VDU system are very different. In an environment where a complete 'HELP' frame can be flashed up in a couple of seconds the big danger is not one of slowing the system down, but of swamping the inexperienced user with information. Keep screen panels reasonably simple, and avoid highlighted or reverse-video fields unless you want a very strong emphasis. Rather than putting everything on the same screen, split things over three or four screens, and use PF keys to switch between them. Keep the bottom couple of lines free for notes on what the PF keys do, and reserve one PF key (always the same one, obviously) to switch to a 'HELP' frame. Don't use wordy error messages for simple things like non-numeric data – it is quite adequate to bleep the screen, highlight the offending field, and plonk the cursor back under the offending character. Keep to a consistent set of PF keys for things like 'previous page', 'next page', and 'quit'. Set the screen up to make the best use of any hardware tab keys, e.g. if there is a 'tab to top left' key then use this field consistently for your command area.

I'm not sure how much of this really qualifies as 'user documentation'. In many ways a well thought out full-screen system, particularly one which involves a fairly complex editor, is so much more straightforward than the teletype equivalent that most of the traditional 'HELP' material can be quietly forgotten about.

So to the external user documentation, and this chapter finally enters the home straight. The section itself divides into three topics: using the hardware; using the system; and what to do when something goes wrong.

First, the hardware, and very important it is too. It's all too easy to tell a user ' . . . just type)LOAD FRED and you'll be away . . . ' without realizing that most APL keyboards have at least two sets of ')', some ']' and possibly even the odd '}' to add to the confusion. The first thing to appreciate is that a user may not even be familiar with an ordinary typewriter, let alone the considerable sophistication of a VDU keyboard. If you can arrange a formal keyboard training session through, for example, the data preparation department, then do so. A couple of hours under the wing of an experienced teacher will be enough to give anyone a reasonable feel for the hardware, and one barrier between the user and the system will have been broken down. Incidentally, many APL programmers would probably benefit from a decent keyboard training too! When you are faced with typing in a lengthy 'DESCRIBE' function, then being able to touch-type will both speed the job and cut down the eye-strain. Referring constantly from your notes to your fingers to the screen and back again can be very tiring, and is certainly not good for you! Anyway, that is by the by; the main topic is 'the user and the hardware', and there are a couple more small points I would like to make.

- *Siting of VDUs.* Beware of reflections, particularly from fluorescent lights; if these are aligned parallel to the screen they can cause a particularly irritating flicker. Make sure that everyone knows how to adjust the brightness, contrast and bleeper volume.

- *Log-on/log-off procedure.* Over a dial-up line this is often the hardest part of the whole dialogue. Have a clear crib pinned up near the terminal, but make sure that the password doesn't get pencilled in by someone!

- What to expect when the system goes down, and who should be rung up to find out how long the problem is likely to persist.

Finally on this subject, a short true story. Once upon a time a company's VDUs displayed a rather pretty version of the company logo, together with a polite invitation to log on. One day it became necessary to change to a new operating system, and for a short while all the screens said 'THIS TERMINAL IS LOGGED ON TO THE NETWORK SOLICITOR'. On seeing this one occasional user assumed, in all innocence, that the company solicitor had commandeered the entire system! Only after several days' patience did he ring up to find out why!! Moral: just because you have learned to tolerate the meaningless jargon that comes free with the operating system, it doesn't mean that your users have!

Having made sure that all concerned are happy with the keyboard, and know how to log on to the computer, then the next stage is to make them familiar with your system. Perhaps the hardest thing about the system user-guide is finding out if it's actually doing good! So often you lavish several weeks' care and attention on a beautifully produced document, hand it over to the users, and never hear any more about it. Again I feel that the best place for the documentation is *in the workspace*, and that the only things needed in the user-guide are the following:

- A brief explanation of the purpose of the system, and a clear statement of any known limitations. For example in a system to handle critical path networks the user-guide should obviously state the maximum number of activities allowed.

- A clear description of the APL library-management commands where these are relevant to the application.

- A general introduction to the type of dialogue used; for example how to stack commands, how to escape from input loops, and how to ask for help.

- A glossary of the main user-commands, with an example of the use of each. In the case of VDU systems, annotated diagrams of all the screen panels, with some kind of 'map' showing the way related screens link together. A possible notation for such maps is discussed towards the end of Chapter 9.

- Samples of all the reports which the system can generate.

You can go into great detail on the prompts and expected responses for each, but it is probably not necessary given a reasonably friendly dialogue.

Finally then, what to do when things go wrong and you don't have a system which can trap the error. There is an interesting question here as to whether you should lock the main user-functions. If you do, then 'DOMAIN ERROR . . . UP-DATE' isn't a vast amount of help in finding out what went wrong. On the other hand, with unlocked functions you are risking the possibility that a user may ignore the 'LENGTH ERROR . . .' and may restart UPDATE. If it is wrong first time, it will certainly be wrong second time, and it may be progressively corrupting precious data. If the workspace is then saved, with two or three crashed functions on the stack, you may have a pretty tricky recovery job ahead of you!

I think the best plan is probably to leave things unlocked, but to lay down a firm warning that persistence in the face of an APL error-message (particularly one like WS FULL) is dangerous. The best plan is probably to save the crashed workspace as it stands with a name such as 'ZAP'; to log off; and to ring for help. It's a procedure the user should never need, but one that you should make sure he knows.

At that point, I think the time has come to call a halt. Documenting in APL may not be quite as good for the soul as documenting a conventional system, but it is still a bit of an uphill struggle. Now for a bit of blessed relief (for the author as well as the reader!) as we move back to APL itself.

Chapter 8

Useful functions and common idioms

After much thought, I have come to the view that there is no sensible way to arrange this chapter. Related idioms are often used in totally unrelated applications, and similar applications require an incredible diversity of idiom. Thus, rather than attempting to group the material either by idiom, or by application, I am simply going to plough through the APL primitive functions in the conventional 'reference card' order, giving a selection of the idioms relevant to each.

Idioms containing more than one function will normally be included only against the first occurrence, but may occasionally get a cross-reference from the others. Operators (e.g. Scan) are not treated separately, i.e. '<\' will be found under '<', not under '\'. Having done this, I shall then collect together some idioms which are particularly relevant to the subject of text processing. Although many of the examples are given as small functions, there is obviously no reason why they should not be included directly in your code, rather than called as utilities.

Incidentally, this chapter was put together on an APL terminal using a slightly doctored version of the full-screen editor which is described in Chapter 10. Any code has either been included from tried and tested functions, or (in the case of odd lines of APL) it has been tried out during compilation from within the editor. This should guarantee an absolute freedom from typos in the places where it matters most. If you do find any mistakes, I should be glad to know of them!

+ (Conjugate)

When experimenting with bits of code at the terminal, how about

```
+VAR←expression
```

as a rather easier way to display the result than

```
[]←VAR←expression
```

+ (Plus)

Four idioms are of interest here:

- Plus with a Boolean result, to avoid a branch:

```
SCORE←SCORE+ANSWER=RIGHT
```

- Counting matches in two vectors of equal length:

```
DOUBLES←(?36ρ6)+.=?36ρ6
```

- Projection of stock levels, given opening stock, production, and sales:

```
STOCK←OSTK+(+\PRODUCTION)-+\SALES
```

- Sort a list of words by length of word:

```
LIST←LIST[♥LIST+.≠' ';]
```

− (Subtract)

Often successive elements of a vector might be start and finish times of a production run; to subtract these (i.e. VEC[11] − VEC[10]), thus evaluating the run time:

```
RUNTIME←-/VEC[11 10]
```

X (Signum)

Only one idiom here:

- Range check; to return ¯2 ¯1 0 1 2 for conditions 'below lower limit', 'on lower limit', etc.:

```
RESULT←+/×ARG∘.-LIMITS←LOWER,UPPER
```

X (Multiply)

Again, this has interesting effects when used with a Boolean result:

Bool X VALUE gives VALUE for Bool = one
ZERO for Bool = zero

- To add £5 to all overdue bills:

```
BILL←BILL+5×DATE>DUEDATE
```

To get the position of the right-most ones in a Boolean matrix:

```
      M
0 1 0 0
0 1 1 0

      M⌈.×ι1↓ρM
2 3
```

Another very common requirement is to multiply a matrix by a vector, either by row:

```
RESULT←MAT×(ρMAT)ρVEC
```

or by column:

```
RESULT←MAT×⍉(⌽⍴MAT)⍴VEC
```

÷ (Reciprocal/Divide)

Again, only a couple of expressions, which are probably better classed as programming tricks than idioms proper:

- Sum of parallel resistors:

```
RES←÷+/÷R←R1,R2,R3...........etc
```

- Expressions of the form

$$\frac{A}{B} \times \frac{C}{D} \times \ldots \times$$

can be coded as

```
÷/A,B,C,D...
```

＊ (Raise to Power)

Yet again, this one comes in handy with Booleans:

VALUE ＊ Bool	gives	VALUE	for Bool = one
		ONE	for Bool = zero

- To charge 6% interest on all bills over 6 weeks old:

```
BILL←BILL×1.06＊AGE>6
```

- To select the major diagonal of any array:

```
DIAGONAL←(1＊⍴ARRAY)⍉ARRAY
```

⌈ (Maximum)

- Locate the largest element of a vector:

```
POS←VEC⍳⌈/VEC
```

- Catenate a vector as the bottom row of a matrix, padding either as needed:

```
LEN←(1↓⍴M)⌈⍴,V
M←(((0,LEN)⌈⍴M)↑M),[1] LEN↑V
```

⌊ (Minimum)

- To cover 'Bare Input' and cope with the user backspacing into the prompt by
  accident:

```
    Z←BAREIN STRNG;A
    ----------------
[1]    ⍝UNVALIDATED INPUT ROUTINE FOR CHAR. DATA.

[2]    ⎕←A←,STRNG
[3]    Z←((+/∧\' '=Z)↓ρA)↓Z←,⎕
    ▽
```

⌊ (Floor)

- Sometimes used (along with residue) as a sort of 'poor man's decode'; i.e. if 2005 is really '2 men, 5 days' then

  `MEN←⌊0.001×MENDAYS`

- Also to demote an integer variable (which has somehow become real) to 4 bytes:

  `VAR←⌊VAR`

| (Magnitude, or Absolute Value)

- Rather useful for splitting up fields on the screen, e.g.

  `__2.005|__3.000| ...`

  but apart from that, I am rather scratching my head on this one!

| (Residue)

This comes in very handy when you need to force an incremental process to cycle.

- To dump data on to a set of 20 work files:

  `DUMPΔTO FILENO←1+20|FILENO`

- To throw a new page every 60 lines:

  `±(0=60|LINECT←LINECT+1)/'ΔNEWPAGE PCT←PCT+1'`

- Also there is the other half of the 'Decode' equivalent:

  `DAYS←1000|MENDAYS`

- Finally a distinctly silly way of generating prime numbers (and getting WS FULL if you're not careful):

  `PRIMES←(2=+/0=(⍳N)∘.|⍳N)/⍳N`

⊗ (Base X Log of Y)

When sorting character data, a common technique is to use ⊥ to clump columns together. Because the numeric precision of the computer is finite ($2*31$ is the largest number that can be stored without getting blurred), the number of columns per clump depends on the collating sequence (∆CS).

- For an alphabetic sort (39 characters):

```
+MAXCOLS←⌊(ρ∆CS)⍟2×31
```

5   (10 for 2×56 which some systems allow)

! (Binomial)

Well, if you're feeling particularly peeved with the world and want to write some really obscure code, how about

Boolean ! VALUE   gives   ONE   for Bool = 0
                            VALUE   for Bool = 1

Apart from that, I don't really think that this rather specialized mathematical function lends itself to idiomatic use!

< (Less Than)

- Are any values below minimum limit?

```
WARN←STOCK∨.<MINSTOCK
```

- Useful effect on Boolean vectors of leaving only the left-most '1' switched on:

```
     <\0 0 1 0 1 1 1
```

0 0 1 0 0 0 0
For example, to remove duplicate rows in a table

```
MAT←(1 1 ⍉<\MAT∧.=⍉MAT)/MAT
```

or (but marginally less efficient)

```
MAT←(∨≠<\MAT∧.=⍉MAT)/MAT
```

This is one case where a looping approach can be a great deal faster. For tables with large numbers of duplicated rows, the 'all-play-all' method of '∧.=' does an awful lot of redundant comparisons. See Chapter 11 for the exact figures.

≤ (Less Than or Equal to)

- If you use this on Booleans, it will leave only the left-most zero turned off:

```
     ≤\1 1 0 0 1 0
```

1 1 0 1 1 1

- Here is a little function (∆LKP) to find the minimum input needed to identify a command unambiguously:

```
      CL←',' ΔTAB 'ADD,UPDATE,FETCH,FILE'

      CL ΔLKP 'U'
2

      CL ΔLKP 'FE'
3

      CL ΔLKP 'FILL'
5                              i.e. not found

      CL ΔLKP 'F'
5                              also not found, being ambiguous


      POS←TABLE ΔLKP CMD;M
      --------------------

[1]   ⍝FIND UNAMBIGUOUS REFERENCES TO CMD IN TABLE.

[2]   M←((ρTABLE)ρ(1↓ρTABLE)↑CMD)=TABLE
[3]   M←(ρ,CMD)≤+/∧\M
[4]   →(0⌈¯1++/M)↑0,POS←1+ρM
[5]   POS←M⍳1
      ∇
```

- To create an upper triangular matrix:

```
MAT←(⍳N)∘.≤⍳N
```

≥ (Greater Than or Equal to)

The '∘.≥' construction has obvious application in drawing histograms, e.g.

```
HIST←' ⎕'[1+VEC∘.≥⍳⌈/VEC]
```

but these histograms can do rather more than meets the eye.

- The well known vector-to-matrix conversion

```
      ',/' ΔTAB 'FRED,JOE/HARRY,,X'
FRED
JOE
HARRY

X
```

can be achieved with

```
      MAT←DELIM ΔTAB VEC;POS
      ----------------------

[1]   ⍝TURNS A VECTOR INTO A TABLE,
[2]   ⍝BREAKING IT AT GIVEN DELIMITERS

[3]   VEC←VEC,1↑DELIM
[4]   VEC←(~POS←VEC∊DELIM)/VEC
[5]   POS←POS/⍳ρPOS
[6]   POS←POS-1+0,¯1↓POS
[7]   POS←POS∘.≥⍳⌈/0,POS
[8]   MAT←(ρPOS)ρ(,POS)\VEC
      ∇
```

● Or to mimic compression on a matrix,

```
      1 0  1 0 1 ∆COMP ABCDE
      1 1  0 0 0       FGHIJ
ACE
FG
```

where the rows are padded with zeros or blanks as appropriate:

```
      R←MASK ∆COMP MAT;LEN
      --------------------

[1]   ⍝MIMIC COMPRESSION ON RANK 2 ARRAYS : PADS R
[2]   ⍝WITH ZEROS OR BLANKS AS REQUIRED.

[3]   LEN←⌈/+/MASK
[4]   R←(,(+/MASK)∘.≥⍳LEN)\(,MASK)/,MAT
[5]   R←((1↑⍴MAT),LEN)⍴R
      ∇
```

In both these examples, a histogram is created, then ravelled, to generate the correct number of blanks (zeros) for the subsequent expansion.

= (Equals)

All the inner products (∧.= etc.) are probably better left until they crop up under the left-hand function of the pair. That leaves

● Is OBJ all Boolean valued?

```
∧/,OBJ=OBJ=1
```

● If so, demote it to its most compact form:

```
OBJ←OBJ=1
```

Also of course, the outer product '∘.='. This certainly has no shortage of uses, but first a word of warning. Many quite respectable constructions use

```
1 1 2⍉A∘.?B
```

to generate a large (but redundant) matrix, then select the plane which actually means something. This may look neat, but it does involve the CPU in a lot of unnecessary labour, and is rarely an efficient (as opposed to elegant!) solution.

That said, if you really do want to get a matrix, then the outer product is a very good way of doing it.

- To construct an identity matrix of side *N*:

```
IDENT←(ιN)∘.=ιN
```

- To construct expressions, e.g.

Total OF sales BY area

where SALES and AREA are vectors, one uses '∘.=' as 'by' and '+.×' as 'of':

```
TOTAL←SALES+.×AREA∘.=ιΓ/AREA
```

Or if AREA is a set of pointers into a table:

```
 - - -       - - -                - - -                    - - - - - - -
| S |       | V |               | A |                   | NORTH |
| A |       | A |               | R | ---|------->| SOUTH |
| L |       | L |     ....    | E |       |            | EAST  |
| E |       | U |               | A | -->|              | WEST  |
| S |       | E |               |   |                     - - - - - - -
 - - -       - - -                - - -
```

then

```
TOTAL←SALES+.×AREA∘.=ι1↑ρΔAREAREF
```


≠ (Not Equal to)

Again, leaving aside things like 'v.≠' there is one fascinating use of this function, the detailed workings of which never fail to amaze me!

≠\Boolean

has the quite remarkable property of generating a result which flags the parity of the Boolean.

- To remove the bracketed text from a vector:

```
STR←'REMARK(IN BRACKETS),(MORE) ANOTHER REMARK'
M←STRε'()'
(~M∨≠\M)/STRING
```

```
REMARK, ANOTHER REMARK
```

This sort of thing comes in very handy in workspace documentation because, when compiling a function cross-reference, you naturally want to ignore any occurrences of a name within quotation marks. A quick '≠\' works wonders in chopping out all the unwanted bits before the function is searched. Anyway, more on that theme in Chapter 10.

- Another common use of '≠' is to underline headings:

```
H←'CODE DATA DESCRIPTION'
H,[0.5] (H≠' ')\'‾'
```

```
CODE DATA DESCRIPTION
```

- Finally, to check if a Boolean is all ones, or all zeros:

```
CHECK←≠/1 0∈BOOL
```

∧ (And)

Something of an embarrassment of riches on this one! To include all the material under '∧' would rather overload this section, so I'm going to resort to separate sections for '∧.=', '∧/' and '∧\' to make life easier.

∧.= (Table Match)

This has virtually become a compound function in its own right; in fact most APL interpreters treat it as such. Consequently, it tends to execute far faster than you would expect if it really made all those matches before doing the '∧' half! Of course it cheats, and stops as soon as it comes on a mismatch.

- The obvious use is in table lookup:

```
      TABLE
FRED
JOE
HARRY

      (TABLE∧.=5↑'JOE')ι1
2
```

- Or simply to check for a given string:

```
→('END'∧.=3↑INPUT)↑EXIT
```

- Or to remove any completely blank rows from a table:

```
TAB←(~TAB∧.=' ')/TAB
```

- And so on.

∧/ (Are all . . .)

This reads 'Are all . . . conditional expression', and again it cheats. You can easily test this by timing:

```
B←∧/A     for     A←10000↑1     (< 1 ms)
          and     A←10000ρ1     (16 ms)
```

The first expression drops out as soon as it hits a zero, and is again anomalously fast.

- A common use is in validation:

```
→(∧/,TABLE∈' 0123456789.‾')↑ERROR
```

- An interesting sideline is to test whether a vector forms a permutation:

```
TEST←∧/VEC=⍋⍋VEC
```

∧\ (While true)

This has the very useful property of switching off all the 'ones' which occur to the right of the first zero:

```
∧\1 1 1 0 0 1 1 0
```

```
1 1 1 0 0 0 0 0
```

- To left-justify a word list:

```
LIST←(+/∧\LIST=' ')⌽LIST
```

- In a text editor, you might find a command

```
CMD←INSERT/⍝A COMMENT
```

to insert the comment line after the current line of the function being edited. To get rid of the unwanted command (which could have been abbreviated to 'I', 'IN', etc.):

```
1↓(~∧\CMD∊'INSERT')/CMD
```

```
⍝A COMMENT
```

∨ (or)

Not surprisingly '∨\' has very much the opposite effect to '∧\': it turns on any zeros to the right of (or below) the first one:

```
∨\0 0 1 0 0 1 0
```

```
0 0 1 1 1 1 1
```

- To strip leading blanks from a string:

```
STRING←(∨\STRING≠' ')/STRING
```

- To mimic dyadic iota on compatible tables:

```
    POS←B ∆IOTA A
    -------------

[1]    ⍝RATHER SIMILAR TO <<B⍳A>> WHERE B AND A ARE
[2]    ⍝TABLES OF THE SAME WIDTH. IT RETURNS ZERO INSTEAD
[3]    ⍝OF <<1+1↑⍴B>> IF NO MATCH IS FOUND.

[4]    POS←+/∨\⊖<⍀B∧.=⍉A
    ∇
```

. . . often it is more use to get zero for 'not found'.

To illustrate to use of ∆IOTA:

```
CAT           CAT
HAT    ∆IOTA  HAT
HAT           HAT
MAT           FAT
              MAT
```

is

```
1 2 2 0 4
```

If you genuinely want the real thing (i.e. 1 2 2 5 4),

```
POS←(<\(A∧.=⍉B),1)⌈.×⍳1+1↑⍴B
```

will achieve the desired result.

~ (Not)

- Another way of demoting a Boolean object to its most compact form:

```
BOOL←~~BOOL
```

⍲ (Not and, or Nand)

- Removal of leading/multiple blanks from a string:

```
STR←(⁻1↓(M,1)⍲1,M←STR=' ')/STR
```

- '⍲\' to bypass a branch where one of two alternatives must be selected:

```
(⍲\2⍴TEST)/'TRUE ',[0.5]'FALSE'
```

This relies on

```
⍲\1 1    is        1 0
⍲\0 0    which is   0 1
```

⍱ (Nor)

So far, idioms based on peculiar properties of this function have, alas, escaped my net.

? (Deal)

- To shuffle a vector:

```
VEC←VEC[(⍴VEC)?⍴VEC]
```

ρ (Shape of ...)

- Finding the RANK of any APL variable:

```
RANK←ρρVAR
```

- General form for any process which will operate only on vectors:

```
RESULT←(ρMAT)ρ ....process.... ,MAT
```

e.g. character mappings, such as a translation to upper case for non-APL terminals:

```
        UP←ΔUPPER LOW;S1;S2;SWOP;SHAPE;NEW
        ----------------------------------
[1]     ⍝UPPER CASE TRANSLATE.
[2]     S1←'abcdefghijklmnopqrstuvwxyz-'
[3]     S2←'ABCDEFGHIJKLMNOPQRSTUVWXYZ¯'
[4]     SHAPE←ρUP←LOW
[5]     →(+/SWOP←(LOW←,LOW)∈S1)↓0
[6]     NEW←SWOP\S2[S1⍳SWOP/LOW]
[7]     NEW[(~SWOP)/⍳ρNEW]←(~SWOP)/LOW
[8]     UP←SHAPEρNEW
        ∇
```

In a similar vein is the expression to replace a selection of characters in a matrix with blanks:

```
        TEST
___|___|___|45.6|___|34
___ ___ ¯3.4
2   ___|¯5.667 | 56


        (ρTEST)ρM\(M←,~TEST∈'|_')/,TEST

            45.6      34
        ¯3.4
2       ¯5.667    56
```

- Two slightly frowned-upon ways of saving a line of code:

```
   →LAB,ρMAT←..... expression

ERR:→INPUT,ρ□←'INVALID DATA ... PLEASE RETYPE'
```

The second of these is probably fair enough, because (a) it probably never gets executed! (b) it doesn't detract from readability.

- Another idiom which has practically become a language element:

```
⍳ρVEC   or   ⍳1↑ρMAT
```

Examples of this one can wait for iota, but it is again worth noting that many interpreters cheat, and will do '⍳1↑ρMAT' as a single operation without ever going near MAT at all.

- To pick up the last row of a matrix:

```
VEC←MAT[(ρMAT)[1];]
```

- Or to pick up the last column of a matrix:

```
VEC←MAT[;(ρMAT)[2]]
```

as a vector;

```
VEC←MAT[;1↓ρMAT]
```

as a one-column matrix.

A common construction in dialogue is to use null input (i.e. a straight carriage return) to close a cyclic process. This leads to code like

```
_A_GAIN:→(ρCMD←BAREIN 'ENTER COMMAND :- ')↓_D_ONE
                          .
       →_A_GAIN           .
```

for teletype dialogues.

ρ (Reshape)

Along with the monadic 'shape', rho frequently crops up in the general construction:

```
OBJECT←( ..expression.. ρOBJECT)ρOBJECT
```

- To turn either a scalar or a vector into a one-row matrix (leaving rank 2 objects as they are):

```
MAT←(¯2↑1 1,ρOBJECT)ρOBJECT
```

- To turn a vector into a one-column matrix:

```
VERT←((ρVEC),1)ρVEC
```

or

```
VERT←(⌽1,ρVEC)ρVEC
```

or

```
VERT←⍉(1,ρVEC)ρVEC
```

In spite of the double brackets, the first of these is actually the most efficient (marginally) of the three. All are infinitely preferable to

```
VERT←VEC∘.+,0
```

... and anyone caught writing

```
VERT←VEC∘.×,1   or   VERT←0 1↓VEC,[1.5]VEC
```

deserves a summary execution.

Finally, a couple of handy tricks:

- `''ρOBJECT`   selects the first element of OBJECT as a *SCALAR*
- `0=1↑0ρOBJECT` returns 1 for numeric objects, and 0 for character.

ι (Index Generator)

This forms part of many of the most commonly encountered phrases in APL.

- Conditional branch:

  `→LAB×ιA>B`

  See Chapter 4 for the reasons why I don't particularly like this one.

- Find the elements of VEC which fulfil a given condition:

  `POS←( ..expression.. VEC)/ιρVEC`

  `VEC[(~VEC∈'0123456789.')/ιρVEC]←' '`

- Convert a vector of positive integers into a mask:

  `(ι⌈/VEC)∈VEC`

ι (Index of ...)

Again, a fair shoal of useful idioms, many relying on the fact that dyadic iota effectively reverses [. . .], i.e.

  `□AV[□AVιCHARS]`   is   `CHARS`

Because it returns $1 + \rho$VEC, iota can be used to provide default values for unrecognizable input: for example if an abbreviation for a shift may be keyed as 'M', 'A', or 'E', then to assume 'M' as the default

  `SHIFT←'MAEM'['MAE'ιINPUT]`

A similar trick will do a poor man's validation, by substituting zero for non-numeric input:

  `MAT←SHAPEρ±,' 0123456789.0'[' 0123456789.'ιINPUT]`

And to do a complete one-to-one mapping from one character set to another (for instance when writing out EBCDIC data from an APL application):

  `OUTPUT←ΔTRANSLATE[□AVιDATA]`

Some other handy idioms with dyadic iota include the following:

- Removal of duplicates from a vector (either character or numeric):

  `VEC←((VECιVEC)=ιρVEC)/VEC`

- Find the position of the first occurrence of *A* in *B*:

  `POS←⌊/BιA`

ε (Membership)

At this point, my original statement that there was no sensible way to arrange this chapter is proved: I have used up all the idioms for 'membership' already! Although a very powerful function, it is rather specialized and seems less well suited to idiomatic use than some of the more primitive components of APL.

⊤ (Representation in a Number System, or Encode)

- Convert any positive number into a vector (e.g. to calculate a check-digit):

```
VEC←((⌊1+10⊛N)ρ10)⊤N
```

- Separate a real number into integer and fraction:

```
SEP←0 1⊤NUM
```

- Display minutes as hours and minutes:

```
OUTPUT←2⍕0.01×100⊥0 60⊤⌈MINS
```

- Turn a vector of indices into a ravelled array into the coordinates of points in the reshaped form:

```
COORD←1+(ρARR)⊤IND-1
```

(For once I must admit that this looks a great deal neater in zero-origin!) A useful application of this idiom is in full-screen management, because IBM's AP 124 returns the ravelled contents of the screen field which you have read. If the field in question looks like

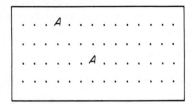

then to find out where the *A*s are:

```
→POS←1+FMT[FLDNO;3 4]⊤⁻1+(INPUT='A')/⍳ρINPUT
```

```
1   3
4   7
```

- Create a truth-table of order *N*:

```
TAB←⍉(Nρ2)⊤⁻1+⍳2*N
```

⊥ (BaseValue, or Decode)

This reverses the action of Encode, and the two functions often occur paired, as in the hours–minutes example just described. On its own, some of its best uses are as follows:

- To right-justify a word list:

```
R←ΔRJUST M
----------
```

```
[1]   ⍝RETURNS A CHARACTER TABLE,
[2]   ⍝ALIGNED ON THE RIGHT MARGIN.

[3]   R←(1-(M=' ')⊥1)⌽M
      ∇
```

This relies on the fact that 'expression ⊥1' does a sort of '+/∧\' from the back:

```
1 0 0 0 1 0 1⊥1
```

```
2
```

- In a similar vein, to strip trailing blanks from a character vector:

```
VEC←(1-(VEC=' ')⊥1)↓VEC
```

- To evaluate a polynomial, e.g. $8x^3 + 2x^2 + 9x + 5$ (traditional notation) for x equal to 10:

```
10⊥8 2 9 5
```

```
8295
```

- To conserve storage, by packing several vectors into one; e.g. to record the activities of 12 crafts, each of which use nine men on a job, for 100 days:

```
ΔDATA←13 10 101⊥ΔCRAFT,[1] ΔMEN,[1.5] ΔDAYS
```

Obviously, the packing can be reversed with an equivalent Encode. Personally, I dislike this method because (a) it uses a fair whack of CPU; (b) it makes ΔDATA totally meaningless, leading to severe debugging problems.

- To perform a 'scattered point' selection from an array:

```
□←MAT←',' ΔTAB 'CLUB,DIAMOND,HEART,SPADE'
```

```
CLUB
DIAMOND
HEART
SPADE
```

```
MAT ΔSPS 5 2⍴ 4 1,1 3,2 2,3 5,4 1
```

```
SUITS
```

```
R←MAT ΔSPS COORD;SHAPE
----------------------
```

```
[1]   ⍝SCATTERED-POINT SELECTION ON MATRIX OF ANY RANK.
[2]   ⍝<<MAT>> IS THE TARGET ARRAY
[3]   ⍝<<COORD>> IS A TABLE OF REQUIRED POINTS, WITH A
[4]   ⍝          COL FOR EACH DIMENSION IN <<MAT>> AND
[5]   ⍝          ROW FOR EACH POINT TO BE SELECTED.

[6]   SHAPE←⍴MAT
[7]   R←(,MAT)[(SHAPE⊥(1⌽⍳⍴⍴COORD)⍉COORD)+1-SHAPE⊥1]
      ∇
```

This last is effectively a reversal of the Encode example which deduced the coordinates in a ravelled matrix. The skeleton form is:

```
POS←1+(ρMAT)⊥COORD-1
```

- Finally, a general vector-to-matrix reshape, where I for once have given in to zero-origin!

```
      ρMAT←'/,' ΔARRAY 'FRED,2,XX/JOE,,ZZZ'

2 3 4

      MAT[1;;]

FRED
2
XX
```

The original of this splendid *tour de force* is due to Andreas Werder of I.P. Sharp (Zurich) and was first seen (in a slightly different style) in the UK APL user-group newsletter of December 1979:

```
      R←DEL ΔARRAY STR;⎕IO;P;SHAPE;MASK
      --------------------------------┬--

[1]   ⍝GENERAL VECTOR TO MATRIX RESHAPE.
[2]   ⍝DEL IS A HIERARCY OF DELIMITERS.
[3]   ⍝STR IS A CHAR VECTOR DELIMITED BY THESE.
[4]   ⍝<< R >> HAS RANK (1+ρ,DEL)

[5]   ⎕IO←0
[6]   R←0,(,DEL)∘.=STR
[7]   P←∨⍀((¯1↑ρR)↑1),[0] R
[8]   R←+\R,[0]~(¯1,¯1↑ρR)↑P
[9]   R←R-⌈\P× 0 ¯1 ↓0,R
[10]  SHAPE←1+⌈/R
[11]  MASK←(⍳×/SHAPE)∊SHAPE⊥R
[12]  R←((-ρSHAPE)↑1)↓SHAPEρMASK\' ',STR

[13]  ⍝A SMALL PRIZE IS OFFERED TO THE FIRST PERSON TO
[14]  ⍝EXPLAIN HOW THIS WORKS!!    ACDS MAY 80.

      ∇
```

⌽ and ⊖ (Reverse and Rotate)

Again, I have already used up a lot of the idioms for these; however, there are a couple left in the bag:

- Here is an interesting use of rotate with a Boolean to exchange the arguments of any scalar function:

```
*⌿( ..conditional expression..) ⊖A,[0.5] B
```

which performs $A*B$ or $B*A$ depending on the condition.

- When producing the function listings used in this book, I have used an idiom to rotate any labels into the left-hand margin:

```
    LAB:STATEMENT
         STATEMENT
    LONGLAB:STATEMENT
```

```
ALOCATE COLONS WHICH OCCUR BEFORE QUOTES OR A'S

R←+/v\φ<\3=L\'A'':'ιFN

AROTATE LABELS AND A TO STAND OUT TO THE LEFT

FN←Rφ(-⌈/0,R←R+FN[;1]='A')φFN
```

⍉ (Transpose)

This can often be used to refine a result by selecting the meaningful plane from a large array of redundant data.

- An alternative approach to the scattered-point selection (△SPS) is

```
    1 1 ⍉MAT[1 2 4 3 1;1 3 2 5 1]
```

SUITS

- To multiply each row of a table by a vector:

```
TAB←1 2 1⍉MAT∘.×VEC
```

Both these examples are fine for small arrays, but will really chew up the CPU if used indiscriminately! APL isn't clever enough to know in advance that you only want a tithe of the selected data, so it will waste an awful lot of time working out redundant figures.

↑ and ↓ (Take and Drop)

For a discussion of branching, see Chapter 4. A selection of other uses is as follows:

- Pad an array up to 133 chars for printing:

```
MAT←(0 133⌈ρMAT)↑MAT
```

- Create a matrix of blanks (zeros) except for the value in one corner:

```
MAT←10 80↑'1'
```

- Create a singleton of rank N:

```
(Nρ0)↑ ..scalar
```

- Remove rows D for N from a matrix (i.e. DEL 5/2 in an editor, with DEL 5/99 meaning 'to the end'):

```
MAT←(~(1↓ρMAT)↑((D-1)ρ0),Nρ1)/MAT
```

- A rather handy little function for teletype dialogues, called STACK, which I haven't managed to fit in anywhere else:

```
    CMD←STACK STRNG;A
    ----------------

[1]        ⍝GENERAL PURPOSE COMMAND STACK

[2]            →(ρSTK←(⌊/STKιDELIM)↓STK)↑BYPASS
[3]            ⎕←STRNG
[4]            STK←(ρSTRNG)↓,⎕
[5]    BYPASS:STK←(~∧\STKεDELIM)/STK
[6]            CMD←¯1↓(⌊/STKιDELIM)↑STK
        ▽
```

The usage of this is quite well illustrated in the section on refining the dialogue in Chapter 6, or by an example such as

COMMAND : ALTER/FRED/JOE 1/99,DEL 3/2,FILE

where a succession of commands is stacked up, separated by commas:

```
    FN;DELIM;STK;CMD
    ----------------

[1]        ⍝TO TEST COMMAND STACK

[2]            DELIM←',',STK←''
[3]    INPUT:→(ρCMD←STACK 'ENTER COMMAND :- ')↓EXIT

[4]        ⍝PROCESS COMMAND

[5]            ⎕←CMD
[6]            →INPUT
[7]    EXIT:'READY'
        ▽
```

The prompt is only redisplayed when the stack of commands is exhausted. Multiple delimiters are ignored, except at the end of an input line; in this case a null command is returned, terminating the dialogue.

⊞ (Domino)

Not an operator that I personally have used a great deal; however, it does make for easy regressions:

COEFF←B⌹1,[1.5] A

[...] Indexing

I suppose this qualifies as a function - anyway, it's far too interesting to leave out! The three idioms given here do little more than scratch the surface, and I'm sure you will find that those rather mundane square brackets offer a superb range of creative possibilities.

- ● Efficient removal of duplicates when a large target vector has a known range of positive integer values:

```
INT←999ρ0
INT[TARGET]←1        allowed range is 1-999
R←INT/ιρINT
```

- A 'ditto' function for character tables. This sort of thing can save a lot of time in full-screen mode:

```
     R←CH ΔDITTO MAT;DT
     ------------------

[1]   ∩REPRODUCES PREVIOUS LINE WHEN 'CH' FOUND.

[2]   DT←,MAT[1⌈⌈\(~MATν.=CH)×ι1↑ρMAT;]
[3]   R←(ρMAT)ρ(DT,,MAT)[(ιρDT)+(ρDT)×,~MAT∈CH,' ']
     ∇
```

```
'=' ΔDITTO      FRED BLOGGS   ======>>   FRED BLOGGS
                =  HARRIS                FRED HARRIS
```

- Finally, a kind of 'scattered-point' assignment, using a combination of Decode and Indexing. It is illustrated here by a simple scatter-plot:

```
     MAT←Y SCATTER X;SHAPE;POS
     -------------------------

[1]   ∩BASIC SCATTER PLOT OF TWO VARS.

[2]   MAT←,(SHAPE←(⌈/Y),⌈/X)ρ' '
[3]   POS←1+SHAPE⊥¯1+Y,[0.5] X
[4]   MAT[POS]←'*'
[5]   MAT←⊖'+',[1] SHAPEρMAT
     ∇
```

⍋ and ⍒ (Grade)

Grade really is an exceptionally clever and subtle concept. The obvious approach would have been to provide a SORT function which, when applied to a vector, would put it into sequence. By stopping halfway, grade makes simple ordering marginally harder, but in the process provides APL with a marvellous range of idioms for ranking, ordering, and selecting.

- To start with the obvious one:

```
V←V[⍋V]   or   V←V[⍒V]
```

will sort a numeric vector into ascending or descending sequence.

The beauty of GRADE is that it can be used to rearrange objects other than the one from which it was generated, e.g. personnel sorted by age can be achieved with

```
PERSONNEL[⍋AGE]
```

- To sort a matrix by column *N*:

```
MAT←MAT[⍋MAT[;N];]
```

- To sort a matrix by all the columns (treating the left-most as the major key), two approaches are possible. Decode can be used to combine all the columns as a vector:

```
MAT←MAT[⍋(0,1+⌈/0 1↓MAT)⊥⍉MAT;]
```

e.g. to sort a table of dates (three columns which are respectively YR, MONTH, DAY):

```
DATES←DATES[⍋0 12 31⊥⍉DATES;]
```

In this case, the decode radix can safely be embedded in the code, since we know in advance the maximum possible range in each column. An alternative is to do an iterative sort, taking the least significant key first:

```
      SORTED←∆NSORTU MAT;GR;COL
      --------------------------

[1]        ⍝SORT NUMERIC ARRAY BY COL.

[2]        COL←(ρMAT)[2]
[3]        GR←⍳1↑ρMAT
[4] LOOP:→COL↓EXIT
[5]        GR←GR[⍋MAT[GR;COL]]
[6]        →LOOP,COL←COL-1
[7] EXIT:SORTED←MAT[GR;]
      ▽
```

Even though this avoids rearranging the data until the last minute, it is still slower than the Decode approach. However, there is no other easy way out when the value of the encoded keys may exceed 2*31.

So far, this discussion of Grade has been based entirely on numeric objects. Several new implementations of APL have extended its domain to character vectors, and even character tables. However, for the moment the rest of us must be content with a further shoal of idioms, in which Grade is joined by dyadic iota.

The collating sequence is often just

```
      ∆CS←' ABCDE .........XYZ0123456789', .. odds n' ends
```

but not always; it might be 'CDEFGAB' for the musical scale; 'CDHS' for a hand of cards; 'IVXLCDM' for Roman numerals; or many other possibilities.

- To sort a Bridge hand:

```
      HAND

K45QT
HSCCC
```

first by suit

```
      HAND[;⍒'CDHS'⍳HAND[2;]]

4K5QT
SHCCC
```

then by denomination

```
HAND[;♥'23456789TJQKA'ιHAND[1;]]
```

KQT54
HCCCS

or by both (denomination within suit)

```
MINORΔKEY←♥'23456789TJQKA'ιHAND[1;]
HAND[;MINORΔKEY[♥'CDHS'ιHAND[2;MINORΔKEY]]]
```

4KQT5
SHCCC

• A more usual requirement is a straight alpha sort of a name list. Again the Decode approach is fine if you don't mind a loss of precision after the first five or six columns:

```
SORTED←NAMES[Δ(ρΔCS)⊥ΔCSι⍉NAMES;]
```

To get over this problem, we could simply revert to a column-by-column sort, but why not let Decode bite off as much as it can chew at each iteration? Remembering the MAXCOLS idiom:

```
      GR←CS ΔCGRADEU MAT;COL;COLS;BASE;MAXCOLS
      ------------------------------------------
[1]        ⍝REASONABLY SLICK MIMIC OF ASCENDING GRADE.

[2]        COL←(ρMAT)[2]
[3]        GR←ι1↑ρMAT
[4]        BASE←2⌈1+ρCS
[5]        MAXCOLS←⌊BASE⍟2*31
[6]  LOOP:→COL↓0
[7]        COL←COL-COLS←COL⌊MAXCOLS
[8]        GR←GR[ΔBASE⊥¯1+CSι⍉MAT[GR;COL+ιCOLS]]
[9]        →LOOP
      ∇
```

This could either be used 'in the raw', or could be called by an alphabetic sort routine such as

```
      SORTED←ΔALPHSORT MAT;CS
      ------------------------
[1]   ⍝SIMPLE ALPHABETIC SORT

[2]   CS←' ABCDEFGHIJKLMNOPQRSTUVWXYZ0123456789'
[3]   SORTED←MAT[CS ΔCGRADEU MAT;]
      ∇
```

• Sometimes we want to sort the rows of a numeric table independently:

```
      ΔROWSORT 2 6ρ 3 1 3 2 5 5, 2 1 1 3 1 5
```

1 2 3 3 5 6
1 1 1 2 3 5

A function to do this is

```
SORTED←ΔROWSORT MAT;GR;SHAPE
----------------------------

[1]   ⍝SORT EACH ROW OF MAT IN ASCENDING ORDER.

[2]   SHAPE←⍴MAT
[3]   MAT←,MAT
[4]   GR←⍋MAT
[5]   SORTED←SHAPE⍴MAT[GR[⍋⌈GR÷SHAPE[2]]]
      ∇
```

which uses the second element of the shape as the major key, the data itself as the minor key.

One theme which permeates all this discussion on sorting is the need to avoid rearranging data unless this is absolutely necessary. In the context of a dialogue, one might have

SELECT   sets up ΔSEL as the indices of the required data

SORT   rearranges ΔSEL

REPORT   displays the data, indexed by Δ SEL

where SORT, rather than ordering the data directly, simply rearranges a global variable which is then used by the REPORT to print/display the data in the required order. Obviously, ΔSEL must be set to a sensible value when the workspace is loaded.

Enough, anyway, of sorting. Other uses of GRADE include the following:

● *Selection*

```
VEC[3↑⍒VEC]     the three largest elements of VEC in descending order

((⍋⍒VEC)∊⍳N)/VEC    the N largest (in the order they occur in VEC)

((⍋⍋VEC)∊⍳N)/VEC    the N smallest
```

● *Ranking*

```
⍋⍒     gives a descending rank vector
⍋⍋     gives an ascending rank vector
```

This comes in very handy when you want to merge two vectors, using a Boolean to interleave the elements:

```
VOWELS←'AEIOUY' <> CONS←'BSTMSL'

MERGE←0 1 1 1 0 1 0 0 0 1 1 0

(VOWELS,CONS)[⍋⍋MERGE]

ABSTEMIOUSLY
```

● *Reporting.* In the foreign currency log I mentioned in Chapter 7, it would be very nice to have the reports sorted by currency, and by amount. Since we can't do both at once, a good second best is to sort by currency, and to display the RANK of the amount as an additional column in the report.

```
CURRENCY          AMNT(STERLING)        RANK
========          ==============        ====

US. DOLL              3400               3
US. DOLL             24000               1
D. MARKS              4000               2
F. FRANCS              200               4
```

```
TAB←(∆CCYREF[CCYPTR;],10 0▼AMT,[1.5]▲▼AMT)[ORDER;]
```

Having ground through the primitive functions one by one I now want to collect those idioms most relevant to the subject of text-processing. It says something for the generality of APL that a notation devised to express complex mathematical ideas can be so readily adapted to a totally unrelated field.

- Set any occurrences of CHARS to blank:
```
STR←MASK\(MASK←~STR∊CHARS)/STR
STR[(STR∊CHARS)/ιρSTR]←' '
```
- Chop off leading blanks:
```
STR←(∨\STR≠' ')/STR          the neat way

STR←(+/∧\STR=' ')↓STR        the quick way
```
- Chop off trailing blanks:
```
STR←(1-(STR=' ')⊥1)↓STR      the pretty way

STR←(-+/∧\⌽STR=' ')↓STR      the quick way
```
- Compress multiple blanks:
```
STR←(¯1↓M∧1⌽M←0,STR=' ')/STR
```
- Remove/select text within any paired characters:
```
STR←(~M∨≠\M←STR∊'()')/STR       remove

STR←((~M)∧≠\M←STR∊'()')/STR     select
```
- Insert CHARS in STR before/after the positions flagged by the ones in MSK:
```
INS←(,MSK∘.∨0 1)/(2×ρMSK)ρ0 1    before
INS←(,MSK∘.∨1 0)/(2×ρMSK)ρ1 0    after
STR←INS\STR
STR[(~INS)/ιρINS]←CHARS
```
- Pattern match (i.e. where is SUB in TARGET?):
```
POS←(∧/(0,ι¯1+ρSUB)⌽SUB∘.=TARGET)/ιρTARGET
```
or for large strings and big targets:

```
      POS←TARGET ΔSS SUB;LEN;GR;CT
      ----------------------------

[1]        ⍝QUICK STRING SEARCH FOR SUB IN TARGET.
[2]        ⍝ALL LOCATIONS WHERE SUBSTRING IS FOUND.

[3]         TARGET←,TARGET
[4]         SUB←,SUB
[5]    →(2 1 0 ≤ρSUB)/OK,SINGLE,EMPTY
[6]  EMPTY:→0,POS←⍳ρTARGET
[7]  SINGLE:→0,POS←(TARGET=SUB)/⍳ρTARGET
[8]      OK:LEN←0⌈(ρTARGET)-(ρSUB)-1
[9]         SUB←SUB[GR←⍒' ETARINOS'⍳SUB]
[10]        GR←GR-1
[11]        →(ρPOS←(LEN↑GR[1]↓TARGET=SUB[1])/⍳LEN)↓0
[12]        GR←1↓GR
[13]        SUB←1↓SUB
[14]        CT←1
[15]  LOOP:→(ρPOS←(TARGET[POS+GR[CT]]=SUB[CT])/POS)↓0
[16]        →((ρSUB)≥CT←CT+1)↑LOOP
      ∇
```

or to get the row of a table in which a given string occurs:

```
      POS←TABLE ΔSSM STR;SHAPE
      ------------------------

[1]    ⍝LOCATE ROW(S) OF TABLE WHERE STRING OCCURS

[2]     SHAPE←ρTABLE
[3]     POS←(,TABLE) ΔSS STR
[4]     POS←1+SHAPE⊤POS-1
[5]     POS←((POS[2;]≤1+SHAPE[2]-ρ,STR)/POS)[1;]
      ∇
```

- Create a word-list from a sentence:

```
    LIST←UNIQUE ' ' ΔTAB ΔNEATEN INPUT
```

- Right-justify a word-list:

```
    LIST←(1-(LIST=' ')⊥1)⌽LIST
```

- Left-justify a word-list:

```
    LIST←(+/∧\LIST=' ')⌽LIST
```

- Remove blank rows:

```
    LIST←(~LIST∧.=' ')⌿LIST
```

- Find WORD in a word-list:

```
    ROW←(LIST∧.=(1↓ρLIST)↑WORD)⍳1
```

- Sort, using sequence ΔALPH (39 characters):

```
    LIST←LIST[⍋39⊥ΔALPH⍳⍉LIST;]
```

- Sort by length of word:

```
    LIST←LIST[⍒LIST+.≠' ';]
```

- Remove duplicate words from list:

```
LIST←(1 1 ⍉<\LIST∧.=⍉LIST)/LIST
```

- Or for lists with many duplicates:

```
      LIST←UNIQUE MAT
      ----------------

[1]      ⍝RETURN UNIQUE ELEMENTS IN MAT

[2]        LIST←MAT[,1;]
[3]   LOOP:→(1↑⍴MAT←(~MAT∧.=LIST[(⍴LIST)[1];])/MAT)↓0
[4]        LIST←LIST,[1] MAT[1;]
[5]        →LOOP
      ∇
```

- Membership of a new word in a word-list:

```
FOUND←∨/LIST∧.=(1↓⍴LIST)↑WORD
```

- Dyadic iota on two compatible lists:

```
POS←(<\(A∧.=⍉B),1)⌈.×⍳1+1↑⍴B
```

or if you would rather have zero for elements not found:

```
POS←+/∨\⊖<⍀B∧.=⍉A
```

which is probably the strangest-looking sequence of symbols I can ever remember seeing!

Taken together, these idioms make APL quite unexpectedly powerful in text-processing applications. I suspect that, as APL becomes more widespread, such idioms will increasingly be taught as a basic part of the language, and will no longer need to be re-invented by successive generations of APL programmers.

That concludes this chapter on idioms and useful functions. I cannot claim to have invented much of the material, nor is the list by any means complete; however, I hope that by collating it I have made some contribution towards its accessibility and consistency. The question of efficiency I am deliberately leaving aside for the moment; several bits of code will doubtless reappear in Chapter 11 with a much deeper analysis of what is going on 'under the bonnet'. Now a digression into a subject which really is (at least as I write this in 1980) new to APL: full-screen management.

Chapter 9

Full-screen management in APL

For too long, APL has been a multidimensional notation constrained by a one-dimensional view of the world. Even now, life is not perfect: why can't we just treat quad as the screen?

```
□[2+ι3;10+ι60]←HEADING

DATA←□[10+ι10;10+ι20]
```

the damn' thing *looks* like a screen after all! One day . . . ?

For the moment then, we have IBM's AP124 and let us try to make the best of it. In this chapter I want first to give a general review of screen management with AP124, then to tackle in detail the utility functions needed to drive it, and finally to make some general points from my own experience of full-screen dialogues.

First, a short review of what screen management is and does. I am going to refer specifically to the IBM 3270 display system (which bids fair to become a *de facto* standard anyway), but I hope that most of this section will be more generally valid. The simplest possible case would be to define the whole screen as one 24 by 79 matrix. (Again, 24 lines by 80 columns seems usual, although wider screens are eventually beginning to happen.) Because of the way the 3270 system works, you always lose control over the column immediately to the left of any part of the screen you define; that is the reason for 24 by 79, not 24 by 80. Into this 'field', as it is called, you could place a 24 by 79 character matrix, and it would promptly pop up on the screen. This is where the fun begins, because as soon as APL has finished any function it issues six spaces, as its way of saying 'Ready'. To display these spaces the system has to revert to the standard screen format, so no sooner have you created your screen than APL wipes it out for you! The only way round this is to pretend that you want to read the screen, as well as to write to it. Then APL will wait for you to press 'Enter' before it sends out its 'Ready' prompt:

```
FSMΔFMT 1 1 24 79          set up the screen

1 FSMΔW 24 79ρ'RABBITS '   write data to field no. 1

DUMMY←FSMΔHOLD             hold it!
```

The details of what the various 'FSM . . . ' functions do should become apparent as we go along; I shall leave any comments on their innards until the next section.

In its simplest guise, FSMΔFMT takes a four-element vector:

location of top left of field – row
                                  – column

| shape of field | – no of rows |
| | – no of columns |

and defines the screen appropriately.

FSMΔW takes the field number (in this case there is only one) on the left, the field contents on the right and moves said contents into the specified field.

FSMΔHOLD waits for 'Enter' (or 'Clear' or a PF key) and returns a vector indicating the numbers of any fields which have been changed. In this case, there can't be any, for reasons about to be explained!

In addition to telling the 3270 where a field is, and what shape it is, you can also define a field's 'attributes' and its 'intensity'. Those lucky enough to get their hands on a 3279 can also play with different colours, of which more later.

The 'attribute' of a field determines whether or not the terminal will let you type anything into it. The default is 'protected', which means that you can't. To make a field available for input you could either use

FSMΔIN field   i.e.   FSMΔIN 1

or add a fifth element to the original format vector:

FSMΔFMT 1 1 24 79 0

where zero means 'input' and two is the code for 'protected'.
The 'intensity' of a field can be

highlighted	code 2
normal (the default)	code 1
hidden	code 0

Again you could use

2 FSMΔINT fld   e.g.   2 FSMΔINT 1

to highlight a field, or you could define it as highlighted with (you've guessed it!)

FSMΔFMT 1 1 24 79 0 2

the sixth element of the format vector.

One general point before I go on. The only operations which physically (as opposed to logically) alter the screen are

FORMAT	(FSMΔFMT)
WRITE	(FSMΔW)
HOLD	(FSMΔHOLD)
READ	(FSMΔR)

Anything else, such as a change of intensity, or positioning of the cursor, only actually happens when you do one of the above. It is no use doing

```
[1]    DUM←FSMΔHOLD
[2]    FSMΔCU 1
[3]    INPUT←FSMΔR 1
```

and expecting to see the cursor leap to field 1 ready for you to start typing. To achieve this effect, you have to do lines 1 and 2 in backwards order:

```
[1]    FSMΔCU 1           store the cursor move
[2]    DUM←FSMΔHOLD       action the move, and hold
[3]    INPUT←FSMΔR 1      get back the contents of field
```

This 'delayed action' effect is the cause of frequent confusion, and I would suggest that you avoid changing attributes/intensities 'in flight' unless absolutely necessary. That only leaves

Cursor positioning   (FSMΔCU)
Sounding the alarm   (FSMΔBLEEP)

to worry about.

What, then, could you usefully do with the knowledge (and functions) I have introduced so far? Well a simple text-editor is certainly a possibility:

```
       NEWTEXT←EDIT TEXT
       -----------------

[1]        ⍝BASIC TEXT EDITOR
[2]        FSMΔFMT 5↑ 1 1 , 24 79 ⌊⍴TEXT
[3] LOOP:FSMΔCU 1
[4]        1 FSMΔW TEXT
[5]        →(⍴FSMΔHOLD)↓DONE
[6]        TEXT←FSMΔR 1
[7]        →LOOP
[8] DONE:NEWTEXT←TEXT
[9]        FSMΔCLOSE
       ∇
```

To edit chunks of text wider than 80, or deeper than 24, you might use PF keys for scrolling, but the principle is very much the same. Points to note are as follows:

- The cursor is moved back to the top left every time 'Enter' is pressed. This is a good way of showing that the screen is again ready to take input (cf. the six-space indent that I mentioned before).

- If no changes have been made, EDIT assumes this to mean that you have finished.

- FSMΔCLOSE simply retracts and expunges the full-screen shared variables, which were set up by the initial format.

By inserting FMT in lines 2 and 4, and ΔMATEXEC (see later) in line 7 you could turn EDIT into a pretty powerful tool for modifying a numeric matrix; a quick □CR at the top and □FX at the bottom and, hey presto, a full-screen function editor! All this with one field and six utility functions!

Onward to greater things, and to screens with lots of fields, not just one. I don't actually know what the limit on the number of screen fields is. The highest I have ever achieved is 120, which seemed to work happily enough, but anything over

50 is getting pretty exotic, and the screen-design functions (Chapter 10) will only handle up to 53 fields. Setting up multiple fields is simple enough (Figure 9.1):

```
FSMΔFMT 3 4ρ2 35 2 9, 6 10 10 60, 23 5 1 22

1 FSMΔW 'A HEADING',9ρ'='

2 FSMΔW ▼DATA
```

etc.

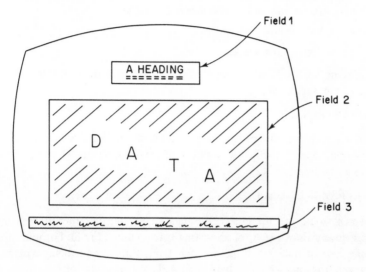

Figure 9.1

Each row of the matrix passed to FSMΔFMT defines a field, just as the vector argument defined a single field. Of course attributes and intensities may also be set. The fields are referred to by their row index in the original matrix, which may incidentally contain rows of zeros; these simply represent unused field numbers. So far, so good, but where are the snags?

- For screens with more than 10 or so fields, screen design becomes a problem, and simple modifications (such as moving fields around) fraught with difficulty. In fact I would never now consider using complex layouts without some suitable software to help with panel editing.

- In its basic form, AP124 takes the ravelled representation of your data, and strings it into the appropriate field with no regard for shape. The expression

```
1 FSMΔW 'A TITLE',[0.5] '='
```

would result in:

```
A TITLE==    not    A TITLE
=====               =======
```

A result not wholly in keeping with expectation!

- Every write to the screen (a) eats CPU – around 20 ms minimum, and (b) causes the screen to flicker. You can get around this by batching up lots of fields into one screen-write:

```
1 2 3 FSMΔW (600↑'A HEADING',9ρ'='),[1]
```

etc. The trouble is that every field must be padded up to the ravelled size of the largest. Most systems restrict shared storage to around 4K, and it's astonishing how easily you can build up to that. In the example above, another four fields – even if only of one character each – and

```
(ι7) FSMΔW (600↑' ........
```

```
SV SPACE QUOTA EXCEEDED
```

or some such helpful message! Again, it's a case of inventing some helpful software, such as (1)

DRAW 'fmtname'

which would allow panels to be sketched on the screen, moved around, deleted, extended, filled with constant text (e.g headings), and given attributes and intensities; (2)

flds FSMΔKEEP data

which would pad up data to the right shape, before either substituting it for previously drawn text, or allocating it to an unused field. For multiple fields, one row of data would go to each field. Rather than being written to the screen, the data would be held in an APL vector, ready for

FSMΔFILL 'fmtname'

which would do a bit of arithmetic to find out the minimum number of

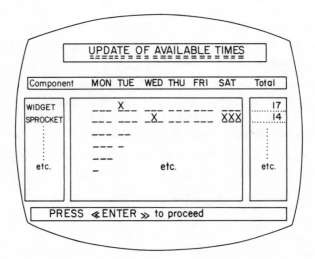

Figure 9.2

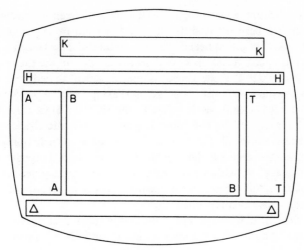

Figure 9.3

screen-writes possible, and would then display any 'drawn' fields which contained text, and any fields which had subsequently been 'kept'.

Before I go into the detail of these, and other, screen-handling functions, here is another example of a possible application. In fact it's the one I referred to briefly back in Chapter 6 when I was talking about full-screen dialogues. The object is to update a 12 by 18 matrix where each element determines whether a particular product can be manufactured on each of the 18 shifts that make up the week. The first stage is to draw a suitable format (DRAW 'FMTBAN'), such as the layout illustrated in Figure 9.2.

Because the fields are sketched on the screen using letters of the alphabet (Figure 9.3), it is obviously convenient to use these letters to identify the fields to the FSM functions (FSMΔCU 'B', etc.).

With this slight refinement in mind, the code to maintain this Boolean table would look something like

```
        BAN;ARR;MASK
        ------------
[1]        ⍝CHANGES DEFAULT COMPONENT BANS,
[2]        ⍝WHICH ARE HELD AS ONES IN ΔBAN.

[3]        FSMΔFMT 'FMTBAN'
[4]        'A' FSMΔKEEP ΔABBR
[5]        MASK←54⍴ 1 0 0 1 0 0 1 0 0
[6]  LOOP:FSMΔCU 'B'
[7]        ARR←MASK\'_X'[1+ΔBAN]
[8]        ARR[;9×⍳6]←' '
[9]        'B' FSMΔKEEP ARR
[10]       'T' FSMΔKEEP 7 0 ⍪ 12 1 ⍴18-+/ΔBAN
[11]       FSMΔFILL FMTBAN
[12]       →(⍴FSMΔHOLD)↓EXIT
[13]       ARR←MASK/FSMΔR 'B'
[14]       ΔBAN←ARR='X'
[15]       →LOOP
[16] EXIT:FSMΔCLOSE
        ∇
```

I hope this illustrates just how powerful the full-screen management can be. I know this wasn't a particularly difficult task, but compare the amount of code in the function 'BAN' with that needed to accomplish the same task in teletype mode. Because the full-screen version is two-dimensional, we can use the positional information (i.e. just where the user typed 'X' on the screen) to deduce the coordinates of ΔBAN into which we must assign zeros. Taking first the user's view: a screen such as Figure 9.2 is clearly vastly easier to use than the most cunningly designed 'bottom-line' approach. Not only does it give an automatic check on the current status, but it also allows all the changes to be made in a single transaction. What's more it removes the need for the user to remember the appropriate abbreviations for the components he wishes to change. Where data editing becomes more complex, this ability of full-screen management to deduce information from an entry's position on the screen becomes invaluable.

Likewise the capability to accept numerous changes at each transaction, and to maintain 'status' fields which are updated every time 'Enter' is pressed. In general, the gain in speed for the user is a factor of between 2 and 5 over 'bottom-line' VDU dialogues; the gain in ease of use is very hard to quantify, but from the enthusiasm with which the changeover to full-screen was greeted, I suspect it was at least as great.

Not forgetting the principle of 'programming by negotiation', I must now consider the system designer's view of the subject! For me, full-screen management has been an enormous step forward, and it has widened considerably the range of applications which APL can realistically hope to tackle. The principal gains have been in the following areas:

- *Economy of code.* APL's matrix-handling really starts to pay off when your input data is two-dimensional, and the size of a typical dialogue function may well fall by over 50%.

- *Clarity of code.* Convoluted expressions to handle stacking or to switch between long and short prompts do nothing for functional elegance.

- *Efficiency of execution.* What were previously many transactions (even with stacking the code still loops) can often be done in one shot. The 'BAN' example uses rather less than one-fifth of the CPU taken by its line-at-a-time predecessor.

- *Speed of design.* Twenty minutes is a good average to set up a fairly complex screen layout. Modification is equally straightforward, and can often be done with the user at your side.

Having enthused for several pages about the marvellous things you can do with screen-management, now back to Earth for a look at how some of those FSM functions actually work.

Driving the Screen

This section deals with the sort of APL functions you will need to make efficient use of IBM's screen management system (AP124). As far as I know, this processor makes no distinction between the various VS APL environments (CMS, CICS, etc.), so although any functions I quote have only been tested under VSPC and CMS, I assume a similar approach will work equally successfully anywhere.

First, why do we need to cover for the raw shared-variable code in the first place? I can think of three main reasons:

- It is not particularly easy to remember what the various screen management codes do; you may be happy writing

  ```
  DATFSM←5 1 1
  ```

  ```
  CTLFSM←1 2
  ```

  but on the whole FSMΔCU 'E' seems rather more meaningful.

- AP124 is distinctly sensitive about the rank and shape of the objects you pass to it. Supposing you wanted to highlight every component where the stock fell below some minimum: what if everything is sufficiently stocked? Unfortunately if you try this with an empty vector of field numbers all you will achieve is a rude return code! Whoever wrote AP124 obviously didn't understand about null vectors!

- It is very easy indeed to do a couple of operations in the wrong order, or to forget to reference the control variable where you should have done. This will leave the auxiliary processor interlocked, which is not at all a nice situation to get yourself (or your user) into.

I hope that makes it clear that no one in his right mind would contemplate writing a serious full-screen application without some suitable software! First, a few design criteria:

- It must take away from the programmer as many of the mundane, time-consuming tasks as possible. Things such as checking that fields do not overlap; padding text to the correct shape; batching as many fields as possible into one screen-write. All these should be done automatically.

- It must lead to readable, easily understood code at the application level.

- It must permit easy modification, for example it should be possible to move a heading without retyping all the text into it.

- It should make reasonably efficient use of the CPU, and ought not to clutter up the workspace with a horde of extraneous variables or functions.

The software that I feel goes some considerable way towards fulfilling these requirements divides naturally into two parts: panel design and panel use. The details of the former would seem to fit better in Chapter 10, but to summarize briefly,

DRAW 'FMTXXX'

creates (or updates if they already exist) two variables: FMTXXX is basically the format matrix already introduced, but it includes one additional column (i.e. seven in all) which consists of indices into FMTXXX△TEXT. This is a character vector containing the text held against each field; an entry of zero in column 7 of the format matrix implies a field with no text.

- Each field is defined in the first place by marking its corners with a letter of the alphabet A-Z, △, A-Z (53 in all).

- Fields may then be moved, extended, deleted, checked for overlap, etc. Attributes and intensities default to Output/Normal, but may be changed by typing 'I' or 'Z' or 'H' in the top left-hand corner.

There is one point here on which I differ from IBM's philosophy – I do not believe in the need to attach labels to fields other than the single letter used to draw them. I know it makes for extremely easy-to-read code:

```
'STOCKS' FSM△KEEP △OSTK
```

but I dislike it for the following reasons:

- It introduces another variable (FMTXXX△LABEL, say). In my view, two is one too many, and three is a downright nuisance.

- It adds another phase to panel design and I like to keep these things as simple as possible.

- It makes hard work of operations involving multiple fields:

```
'PROD,STOCK,SALES' FSM△KEEP 3 20ρ△DATA
```

looks nice, but does take its fair share of CPU in tabulating and looking up the name list. Implicit mapping of fields to variables of the same name would also be possible, but think of the documentation problems! Variables which float from function to function are bad enough, without including the screen in the mystery tour.

Anyway, enough of personal prejudice! If you like the idea of labelled fields, then you can very easily adapt the FSM functions to suit. These screen-using functions fall naturally into five groups:

- FSM△FMT and FSM△CLOSE, which respectively establish and clear up the format.

- FSM△KEEP, FSM△RESET, and FSM△FILL, which update the held text, and move it to the screen.

- FSM△HOLD, FSM△PF, and FSM△PFHOLD, which hold the screen and return various combinations of information on what the user did to it.

- FSM△R, which reads data from the screen.

- FSM△INT, FSM△IN, FSM△OUT, FSM△CU, and FSM△BLEEP, which set up miscellaneous special effects.

Obviously the first thing you must do is to tell AP124 that you want to talk to it, and to pass it your screen layout. This might be done by

```
      FSMΔFMT FMTNAME;FMT;C
      --------------------

[1]          ⍝SHARE FULL SCREEN CONTROL VARS, AND SET UP
[2]          ⍝SCREEN LAYOUT; THEN ESTABLISH FIXED TEXT,
[3]          ⍝ISSUE FORMATTING REQUEST AND SET ATT. AND INT.

[4]          →(1=0=1↑0⍴FMTNAME)↑NUM
[5]          FMT←⍎FMTNAME
[6]          →OFFER
[7]    NUM:FMT←FMTNAME
[8]          FMTNAME←'ΔΔΔΔ'
[9]  OFFER:FMT←(¯2↑ 1 1 ,⍴FMT)⍴FMT
[10]         →(4=×/C←124 ⎕SVO 2 6 ⍴'CTLFSMDATFSM')↑OK
[11]         'NO FSM SHARES' FSMΔERR C
[12]    OK:DATFSM←((1↑⍴FMT),4)↑FMT
[13]         CTLFSM←1
[14]         →(C←CTLFSM)↓ATT
[15]         'FAILED TO FORMAT' FSMΔERR C
[16]   ATT:→(¯1↑⍴FMT← 0 4 ↓FMT)↓TXT
[17]         DATFSM←,FMT[;1]
[18]         CTLFSM←6,⍳1↑⍴FMT
[19]   INT:→(¯1↑⍴FMT← 0 1 ↓FMT)↓TXT
[20]         DATFSM←,FMT[;1]
[21]         CTLFSM←7,⍳1↑⍴FMT
[22]   TXT:→(×⎕NC FMTNAME,'ΔTEXT')↑STORE
[23]         FSMΔKEEP←,' '
[24]         →DONE,FSMΔPTR←(1↑⍴FMT)⍴0
[25] STORE:FSMΔPTR←FMT[;2]
[26]         ⍎'FSMΔKEEP←',FMTNAME,'ΔTEXT'
[27]  DONE:
      ∇
```

Lines 4-8 make the distinction between a named format (FSMΔFMT 'FMTXXX') and a simple numeric argument (FSMΔFMT 1 1 24 79); if the latter, line 8 sets up a dummy name, for reasons soon to become apparent. Lines 9-15 offer the shared variables, and set the basic format. (FSMΔERR simply displays a suitable error message and does a bare right arrow to terminate any calling functions.) Lines 16-18 use column 5 (if it exists!) to set the attributes, lines 19-21 set the intensities similarly. Then for the fixed text, and now we see the reason for that highly improbable name on line 8! Two temporary globals are set up - FSMΔPTR and FSMΔKEEP - which start life as simple copies of column 7 of the format, and the associated ΔTEXT. If this text variable does not exist (i.e. the format was not set up through DRAW, or no text was defined) then FSMΔPTR and FSMΔKEEP are simply initialized (lines 23 and 24).

To get rid of this motley crew of shared and unshared variables,

```
      FSMΔCLOSE;A
      -----------

[1]   ⍝RETRACT FULL-SCREEN VARS, AND ERASE SAME.

[2]   A←⎕SVR 2 6 ⍴'CTLFSMDATFSM'
[3]   A←⎕EX 4 8 ⍴'CTLFSM  DATFSM  FSMΔKEEPFSMΔPTR '
      ∇
```

But before we do that, we obviously want to put them to work! This brings us to

```
        FLDS FSMΔKEEP MAT;FMT;SHAPE;C;NEWFLDS;MAX
        ------------------------------------------

[1]           ⍝BUFFER UP SCREEN FIELDS FOR MULTIPLE WRITE.

[2]           ±(~0=1↑0ρFLDS)/'FLDS←1⌈¯65+⎕AV⍳(FLDS≠' ' ' ')/FLDS'
[3]           CTLFSM←9
[4]           →(C←CTLFSM)↑FAIL
[5]           →(FLDS∨.>1↑ρFMT←DATFSM)↓QK
[6]     FAIL:'KEEP FAILED' FSMΔERR C
[7]       QK:MAT←(¯2↑ 1 1 ,ρMAT)ρMAT
[8]           →(1=ρFLDS←,FLDS)↓MULT
[9]   SINGLE:MAT←(1,×/ρMAT)ρMAT←FMT[FLDS[1]; 3 4]↑MAT
[10]    MULT:SHAPE←×/FMT[FLDS; 3 4]
[11]          →(∨/NEWFLDS←0=FSMΔPTR[[FLDS]])↓REP

[12]          ⍝PAD OUT FSMΔKEEP TO ACCEPT NEW FLDS.

[13]          FSMΔPTR[NEWFLDS/FLDS]←(ρFSMΔKEEP)++\0,¯1↓NEWFLDS/SHAPE
[14]          FSMΔKEEP←FSMΔKEEP,(+/SHAPE×NEWFLDS)ρ' '

[15]          ⍝NOW SUBSTRING TEXT INTO FIELDS.

[16]     REP:MAX←⍳1↓ρMAT
[17]          FSMΔKEEP[1⌈,(SHAPE∘.≥MAX)×FSMΔPTR[FLDS]∘.+MAX]←,MAT
        ∇
```

Basically what this does is to modify two globals, FSMΔPTR and FSMΔKEEP; however, there are one or two slight refinements! Line 2 simply translates field letters ('BCD' FSMΔKEEP . . .) to the corresponding field numbers. Lines 3-5 find out what the current format is, and check that all requested fields fall within it. What happens now depends on whether a single field is being kept, or if FLD is a list of several. Line 9 ensures that the content of a single field is sensibly padded to the right, and down, i.e.

```
     'A' FSMΔKEEP 'TITLE',[0.5]'='

     +-------------------+
     |TITLE              |
     |=====              |
     |                   |
     |                   |
     |                   |
     +-------------------+
```

whereas multiple fields are simply padded to the total size of the corresponding area on the screen (line 10). Line 11 checks whether there is any fixed text held against the field, or if something has already been kept there. If so, the pointer is left as it was and the appropriate chunk of FSMΔKEEP is over-written. Otherwise the pointer is set to the end of the current text and the new text is strung on to the back of FSMΔKEEP.

As a momentary respite from the rigours of all this rather heavy APL; to set the text back to the drawn version,

```
      FSMΔRESET FMT
      - - - - - - - - - - - - -

[1]   ⍝SET SCREEN BACK TO DRAWN VERSION.

[2]   FSMΔKEEP←±FMT,'ΔTEXT'
[3]   FSMΔPTR←(±FMT)[;7]
    ▽
```

which successfully undoes all the hard work of FSMΔKEEP.

The next obvious requirement is to get all that stored text up on the screen; to do this we could use

```
      FSMΔFILL FMT;RANK;THISLOT;MAT;MAX;C
      - - - - - - - - - - - - - - - - - - - - - - - - - - -

[1]     ⍝WRITE HELD FIELDS OUT TO SCREEN.

[2]     ±(~0=1↑0ρFMT)/'FMT←±FMT'
[3]     RANK←⍒×/FMT[; 3 4]
[4]     →(ρRANK←(×FSMΔPTR[RANK])/RANK)↓0'
[5]   NXT:MAX←×/FMT[RANK[1]; 3 4]
[6]     THISLOT←((ρRANK)⌊⌊4070÷MAX)↑RANK
[7]     MAT←FSMΔKEEP[(ρFSMΔKEEP)⌊FSMΔPTR[THISLOT]∘.+ιMAX]
[8]     DATFSM←MAT
[9]     CTLFSM←2,THISLOT
[10]    →(C←''ρCTLFSM)↓OK
[11]    'FIELD NOT WRITTEN' FSMΔERR C
[12]  OK:→(ρRANK←(ρTHISLOT)↓RANK)↑NXT
    ▽
```

No matter how complex the screen, lines 3 and 4 ensure that two screen-writes will be enough to display it; fields are first ranked in order of size, so that the best possible use is made of the available 4K of shared storage. The biggest field determines the number that can be dealt with first time around (of course it may be all the fields), and line 6 holds the field numbers to be taken. Lines 6 and 7 select the corresponding text from FSMΔKEEP (padded up to the size of the largest field, and shaped appropriately). It doesn't matter at all that the text for the smaller fields is padded up with whatever comes next in FSMΔKEEP; this padding never actually makes its way on to the screen. Finally, the padded field contents are passed to AP124, and the fields are written on the screen. If necessary (i.e. there are still some fields remaining) it now loops back to repeat the process.

That basically covers the ways of getting data up on the screen; however, for the sake of completeness I shall include

```
      FLD FSMΔW CHARS;C
      - - - - - - - - - - - - -

[1]     ⍝WRITE TO GIVEN LINE(S) OF SCREEN.

[2]     ±(~0=1↑0ρFLD)/'FLD←1⌈¯65+⎕AVι(FLD≠' ')/FLD'
[3]     →(1 0 =ρFLD←,FLD)/SINGLE,0
[4]     CHARS←(¯2↑(ρFLD),ρCHARS)ρCHARS
[5]     DATFSM←CHARS
[6]     →WRITE
[7]   SINGLE:DATFSM←,CHARS
[8]   WRITE:CTLFSM←2,FLD
[9]     →(C←''ρCTLFSM)↓0
[10]    'FIELD NOT WRITTEN' FSMΔERR C
    ▽
```

This can be used independently of the 'keep-fill' approach to write data directly to screen fields. Its only slight subtlety is line 4, which allows single lines of text (e.g. 'ERROR') to be written to several fields at once.

The next group of functions (FSMΔHOLD, etc.) are concerned with holding the screen you have just created; which one you will want to use depends on the information you want to be returned to you. Several other permutations are possible as well – you might like to discriminate between 'clear' and 'enter', or to find out where the cursor had been left. The principle is the same:

```
    R←FSMΔHOLD;C
    - - - - - - - - - - - -

[1]    ⍝HOLD SCREEN DISPLAY.

[2]    CTLFSM←3
[3]    →((C←DATFSM)[1]∊ 0 1 5)↑OK
[4]    'HOLD FAILED' FSMΔERR C[1]
[5]  OK:R←5↓C
    ∇
```

This tells you which fields have had something typed into them, e.g. if your user has modified fields 'A' and 'R',

```
    FSMΔHOLD

1  18
```

If he has changed nothing at all (or has pressed 'clear'), then

```
    →(ρFSMΔHOLD)↓DONE
```

is a very convenient way of detecting the fact.

```
    R←FSMΔPF;C
    - - - - - - - - - -

[1]  ⍝WAIT FOR INPUT, CHECK THAT A PFKEY WAS
[2]  ⍝USED, AND RETURN NUMBER OF KEY.
[3]  ⍝CLEAR AND ENTER BOTH RETURN 0.

[4]    CTLFSM←3
[5]    C←2↑DATFSM
[6]    R←×/C
    ∇
```

does a similar job, but tells you instead which PF key was pressed.

```
    R←FSMΔPFHOLD;C
    - - - - - - - - - - - - - -

[1]    ⍝WAIT FOR INPUT; IF A PFKEY WAS USED RETURN NO OF KEY
[2]    ⍝OTHERWISE CLEAR AND ENTER BOTH RETURN 0. CATENATE
[3]    ⍝TO THIS THE NUMBERS OF ANY MODIFIED FIELDS

[4]    CTLFSM←3
[5]    →((C←DATFSM)[1]∊ 0 1 5)↑OK
[6]    'HOLD FAILED' FSMΔERR C[1]
[7]  OK:R←(×/2↑C),5↓C
    ∇
```

combines the functions of both the above. The first element tells you which key was pressed, and there are as many remaining elements as there were fields modified.

Having held the screen, and determined that the user has typed something, the next requirement is to retrieve the altered data:

```
      DATA←FSMΔR FLD;C;SHAPE
      ----------------------

[1]        ⍝READ SPECIFIED FIELDS INTO DATA WITHOUT
[2]        ⍝WAITING FOR ENTER OR PFKEY.

[3]        ±(~0=1↑0ρFLD)/'FLD←1⌈¯65+⎕AV⍳(FLD≠' '  '')/FLD'
[4]        CTLFSM←5,FLD
[5]        →(C←''ρCTLFSM)↑FAIL
[6]        DATA←DATFSM
[7]        →(1=ρ,FLD)↓0
[8]        CTLFSM←9
[9]        →(C←''ρCTLFSM)↑FAIL
[10]       SHAPE←DATFSM
[11]       SHAPE←(SHAPE[1]=1)↓SHAPE←,SHAPE[FLD; 3 4]
[12]       →(1=ρρDATA←SHAPEρDATA)↓0
[13]       →0,ρDATA←(1-(DATAε'  _')⍳1)↓DATA
[14] FAIL:'DATA NOT READ' FSMΔERR C
     ∇
```

For multiple fields this simply reverses the action of the screen-write, and returns a padded matrix with one row per field. Single fields are reshaped (lines 8-12), and vector fields have trailing blanks (or underscores) stripped off (line 13):

```
     ρDATA←FSMΔR     +---------------+
                     |FRED BLOGGS    |
                     |JOE SOAP       |
                     |               |
  3 15               +---------------+


                     +--------------------+
     ρDATA←FSMΔR |ADRIAN SMITH_____|
 12 (not 20)         +--------------------+
```

From the point of view of full-screen applications, it is a great shame that APL's execute function works only on vector arguments. This restriction leads us into things like

```
      OUT←ΔMATEXEC MAT;ENT;MASK;ZERO;RHO;P
      ------------------------------------

[1]        ⍝EXECUTE CHARACTER MATRIX,
[2]        ⍝REPLACING INVALID CHARS WITH ZERO.
[3]        ⍝

[4]        MAT←'1234567890 +|_.¯-'⍳MAT
[5]        RHO←ρMAT←' ',('1234567890  _.¯¯0'[MAT]),' '

[6]        ⍝CHOP OUT MULTIPLE UNDERSCORES

[7]        MASK←~(MAT='_')∧1⌽MAT='_'
[8]        MAT←RHOρ(,(+/MASK)∘.≥⍳¯1↑ρMAT)\(,MASK)/,MAT
```

```
[9]      ∩CHOP OUT MISPLACED NEGATIVE SIGNS

[10]     MASK←(MAT≠'¯')∨(MAT='¯')∧(1ΦMAT∈'1234567890.')∧¯1ΦMA
[11]     MAT←RHOρ(,(+/MASK)∘.≥ι¯1↑ρMAT)\(,MASK)/,MAT

[12]     ∩CHOP OUT MISPLACED DEC. POINTS

[13]     MASK←(MAT≠'.')∨(MAT='.')∧1ΦMAT∈'1234567890'
[14]     MAT←(,(+/MASK)∘.≥ι¯1↑ρMAT)\(,MASK)/,MAT

[15]     ∩FIND REMAINING UNDERSCORES

[16]     MASK←('_'=MAT)/ιρMAT

[17]     ∩REPLACE THOSE ON THEIR OWN BY '0'

[18]     ZERO←((MAT[MASK+1]=' ')∧MAT[MASK-1]=' ')/MASK
[19]     MAT[ZERO]←'0'

[20]     ∩AND ANY OTHERS BY BLANKS

[21]     MAT[(~MASK∈ZERO)/MASK]←' '
[22]     MAT←RHOρMAT

[23]     ∩COUNT HOW MANY NUMBERS PER LINE;
[24]     ∩SKIP THE ± IF NONE ANYWHERE.

[25]     →((OUT←0)∧.=ENT←+/MASK∧1Φ~MASK←MAT=' ')/SK

[26]     ∩REMOVE MULTIPLE DEC POINTS FROM EACH NUMBER

[27]     MAT←(~P←MAT=' ')/MAT←,(MAT),' '
[28]     MAT←' ',(ρP)ρ(,P+P∘.≥ι⌈/0,P←(×P)/P←P-1+0,¯1↓P←P/ιρP)

[29]     ∩EXECUTE AND EXPAND TO CORRECT SHAPE

[30]     OUT←(,ENT∘.≥ι⌈/,ENT)\±(,(MAT≠'.')∨<\MAT='.')/,MAT
[31]   SK:OUT←((ρENT),⌈/0,,ENT)ρOUT
       ∇
```

the action of which is best illustrated by

```
+DATA←∆MATEXEC   ____ _20_ ___3 _5__
                 ¯¯¯¯¯¯¯¯¯¯¯¯¯¯¯¯
                  XX  ____ _45.6
```

```
0    20    3      5
0     0   45.6    0
```

Basically it makes the best sense that it can of the screen. Invalid characters are replaced by zeros, as are blocks of contiguous underscores. Each row is padded to match the row with most entries in it; each plane likewise if it is called with an argument of more than two dimensions.

To reverse the effect (i.e. to display a matrix on the screen in a form suitable for updating):

```
R←FMT DFMT MAT;POS;SHAPE;WID;ZEROS;MASK
----------------------------------------

[1]   ∩FILLS DATA FIELDS UP WITH UNDERSCORES FOR F.S. DISPLAY
[2]   ∩RANK OF RESULT IS SAME AS RANK OF RIGHT ARGUMENT.
```

```
[3]    MAT←((-2⌈⍴⍴MAT)↑ 1 1 ,SHAPE←⍴MAT)⍴MAT

[4]    ⍝EXTEND FORMAT STRING AS NEEDED

[5]    FMT←(2×⌈0.5×⍴,FMT)↑FMT
[6]    FMT←((¯1↑⍴MAT),2)⍴FMT

[7]    ⍝REMEMBER SHAPE FOR FUTURE REFERENCE.

[8]    SHAPE←(¯1↓SHAPE),¯1↑⍴R←(,FMT)⍕MAT

[9]    ⍝CHECK FOR LARGEST FIELD.

[10]   WID←⍳1⌈⌈/FMT[;1]-1

[11]   ⍝FIND THE PLACES CORRESPONDING TO ZEROS IN MAT.

[12]   ZEROS←,⍉((⌈/0,WID),⍴,MAT)⍴MAT=0

[13]   ⍝FIND REMAINING FIELDS IN RAVELLED STRING.
[14]   ⍝FIELDS OF WIDTH 1 GET FILLED IN THEIR ENTIRETY.

[15]   POS←(¯1↓2++\0,FMT[;1])∘.+WID-1⌈3-⍴WID
[16]   POS←(MASK←,(1⌈FMT[;1]-1)∘.≥WID)/,POS
[17]   ZEROS←((⍴ZEROS)⍴MASK)/ZEROS
[18]   POS←,((0,⍳¯1+×/¯1↓⍴R)×¯1↑⍴R)∘.+POS
[19]   R←,R
[20]   R[(ZEROS∨' '=R[POS])/POS]←'_'
[21]   R←SHAPE⍴R
       ∇
```

Between them, these two functions provide the basis for any application which involves editing numeric data. (Those of you with a ⎕FMT should be able to concoct DFMT rather more efficiently.)

Finally, a group of miscellaneous functions to do those occasional odd jobs not covered so far:

```
       INT FSM∆INT FLD;C
       -----------------
[1]    ⍝SET GIVEN FIELDS TO REQUIRED INTENSITY

[2]    →(0=⍴,FLD)↑0
[3]    ±(0=0=1↑0⍴FLD)/'FLD←1⌈¯65+⎕AV⍳(FLD≠'' '')/FLD'
[4]    DATFSM←0⌈2⌊INT
[5]    CTLFSM←7,FLD
[6]    →(C←CTLFSM)↓0
[7]    'FIELD MOD FAILED' FSM∆ERR C
       ∇
```

changes field intensities, for example to highlight components out of stock, or overloaded machines.

```
       FSM∆IN FLD;C
       ------------
[1]    ⍝SET GIVEN FIELDS TO ACCEPT INPUT

[2]    →(0=⍴,FLD)↑0
[3]    ±(0=0=1↑0⍴FLD)/'FLD←1⌈¯65+⎕AV⍳(FLD≠'' '')/FLD'
[4]    DATFSM←0
[5]    CTLFSM←6,FLD
[6]    →(C←CTLFSM)↓0
[7]    'FIELD MOD FAILED' FSM∆ERR C
       ∇
```

and

```
FSMΔOUT FLD;C
------------

[1]   ⍝SET GIVEN FIELDS TO REFUSE INPUT.

[2]   →(0=⍴,FLD)↑0
[3]   ±(0=0=1↑0⍴FLD)/'FLD←1⌈¯65+⎕AV⍳(FLD≠' ' ' ')/FLD'
[4]   DATFSM←2
[5]   CTLFSM←6,FLD
[6]   →(C←CTLFSM)↓0
[7]   'FIELD MOD FAILED' FSMΔERR C
    ∇
```

change the protection of fields; for example certain users may not be allowed to
update particularly critical information, at least until they have supplied a password. The appropriate fields can then be unlocked.

```
FSMΔCU FLD;C
------------

[1]    ⍝SET CURSOR POS. DEFAULT IS START OF FLD GIVEN.

[2]     ±(~0=1↑0⍴FLD)/'FLD←1⌈¯65+⎕AV⍳(FLD≠' ' ' ')/FLD'
[3]     →(4⌊⍴,FLD)⌽0,L1,L2,WR
[4]   L1:→WR,FLD←FLD, 1 1
[5]   L2:FLD←FLD[1],1,FLD[2]
[6]   WR:DATFSM←FLD
[7]     CTLFSM←12
[8]     →(C←CTLFSM)↓0
[9]     'CURSOR NOT SET' FSMΔERR C
    ∇
```

gets the cursor to where you want it. It assumes 'top left' unless you specify otherwise, in which case you have to use the field number, rather than letter.

```
FSMΔBLEEP
---------

[1]   ⍝SOUND BLEEP AT NEXT SCREEN I/O.

[2]   CTLFSM←11
    ∇
```

is self-explanatory. If your screen doesn't have an 'audible alarm' it obviously won't
make any noise, but neither will FSMΔBLEEP actually fall over.

   That concludes this section on 'Driving the Screen'. I have, for once, included
a lot of detailed code. This is not because I'm particularly proud of it, on the contrary, many of the functions were put together in rather a hurry and can doubtless
be improved upon. Rather I wanted to illustrate the sort of problems one comes
up against when handling a full-screen application, and to show that they can be
overcome without an enormous amount of effort. I now want to move away from
the nitty-gritty of CTLFSMs and DATFSMs for a few closing thoughts on:

What Makes a Good Full-screen Dialogue?

There are two important things to get right: (a) the design of each screen and (b) how the screens are linked together.

The design of individual screens is obviously more an art than a science, and does depend heavily on the nature of the application. Some of the points which seem to me to be generally valid are as follows:

- Put the most commonly used fields somewhere near the middle.

- Don't use highlighting for small fields, unless they are tucked away in the corners. One highlighted field in the wrong place can make it virtually impossible to concentrate on several nearby fields.

- Where there are several similar-looking screens (e.g. ADD, UPDATE, and DISPLAY) which do different jobs, make it obvious (e.g. with 'DISPLAY' highlighted top right) which is which.

- When a transaction is complete (e.g. some data has been updated) this too should be made clear, and the message should be left on the screen until the next action by the user.

- Make sure that the layout uses the tab keys sensibly. Tabbing across fields is easy in the 3270 system; tabbing down column fields is not. If necessary you can always transpose your data to ensure that the 'natural' sequence is also the convenient one.

- Leave the bottom line (or two lines) free for assorted help messages, e.g.

    PF 10 for Stock Position, 'ENTER' for Full Menu

- As in the example above, use lower-case letters to help reduce the emphasis of descriptive fields. Lower case is definitely more readable for complete 'help' screens.

- Don't overcrowd screens. Either use PF keys to switch formats, or leave 'occasional' fields at zero intensity, again using a PF key as an 'on-off' switch.

The user should be able to switch from anywhere to anywhere within a series of related screens *without* reverting to a menu each time. When first invoked, the root function should go straight to the most commonly used screen of the set, *not* to the menu. For example, in a production scheduling system, an editor might create displays to (a) change the production plan; (b) display a projected stock; (c) display required components; (d) change some basic parameters, such as shift-level or number of machines available; (e) display a menu of the above four options. Assuming PF1 to PF4 for the four stages (a)–(d) above, PF12 to quit, and 'ENTER' for the menu, such an editor could be driven by

```
EDITOR;LAB;ACTION
- - - - - - - - - - - - - - - - -

[1]        ⍝DRIVER FUNCTION FOR SCHEDULE EDIT

[2]          →1↓LAB←MENU,PLAN,STOCK,COMP,PARM,(7ρMENU),QUIT
[3]    MENU:ACTION←EDΔMENU
[4]      LKP:→LAB[1↓ACTION]
[5]    PLAN:→LKP,ACTION←EDΔPLAN
[6]   STOCK:→LKP,ACTION←EDΔSTK
[7]    COMP:→LKP,ACTION←EDΔCOMP
[8]    PARM:→LKP,ACTION←EDΔPARM
[9]    QUIT:'EDIT CLOSED'
       ∇
```

Each function in the set would be something like

```
ACTION←EDΔPLAN;CTL
- - - - - - - - - - - - - - - - - -

[1]        ⍝EDIT CURRENT PRODUCTION SCEDULE

[2]        FSMΔFMT 'FMTEDΔPLN'

[3]     ⍝
[4]     ⍝

[5]        →(1=ρCTL←FSMΔPFHOLD)↑DONE

[6]     ⍝
[7]     ⍝

[8]    DONE:ACTION←CTL[1]
       ∇
```

Figure 9.4 shows one way of representing the dialogue diagrammatically.

This approach has the great advantage that an experienced user can drive the system efficiently, but a novice is never more than one keystroke from the menu, or from APL. There is nothing more frustrating to a user than knowing where he wants to be in the system, and having to plough through a tree of menus to get there; by building in short cuts you both save his time, and save CPU time.

If response time is a problem, it is a good idea to throw out an immediate 'interim response' into the message field at the bottom of the screen (e.g. '***PFKEY 4 accepted: please wait'). This will at least delay the point at which the user starts pummelling the keyboard!

That really covers all I want to say on full-screen dialogues. To restate some of the most important points:

- The screen is two-dimensional, so take full advantage of the positional information.

- Remember the APL philosophy of parallel processing; plonk everything on the screen and read it all back. Don't mess around taking in one field each time 'enter' is pressed.

- Get yourself some decent software for screen design and screen use.

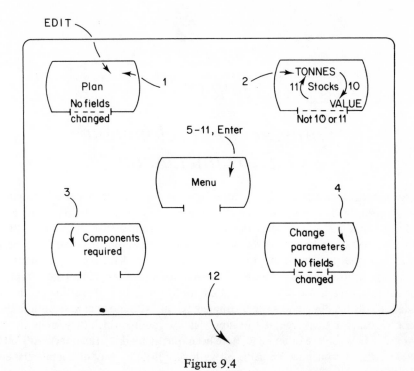

Figure 9.4

- PF keys are a much better way of driving a series of screens than trees of menus.

There remains the intriguing possibility for the future – colour. Many planning applications would undoubtedly benefit greatly from the judicious use of colour screens, and I look forward with considerable anticipation to the day when a book such as this will routinely include a chapter on the use (and abuse!) of colour graphics.

As it is, APL has at long last been granted an input device worthy of its multi-dimensional notation. In the long term this may well be the second crucial factor (file-handling being the first) which will open the gates to an enormously increased range of applications. If this is so, it will not be long before even the most produc-tive APLer is under pressure, and it is in answer to his needs that I move on to soft-ware which is aimed not at the user, but at the programmer himself.

Chapter 10

Software for development and documentation

This chapter is aimed primarily at professional and semi-professional programmers who are using APL to build substantial commercial systems. As befits a pure concept which has lain unnoticed in the backwaters of commercial computing, APL is blessedly free of so many of the sales-inspired 'enhancements' that have been thoughtlessly tacked on to other systems. This freedom has its price, however, in that many facilities which professional programmers take for granted are conspicuously absent from most APLs. When it comes to things like formatting and input validation, file-handling and system commands, the APL bureaux have been falling over each other in their eagerness to supply all the goodies which they know attract customers. IBM, on the other hand, have been quietly marking time; their APL\360 became APLSV, and now VS APL, all with very little by way of commercial enhancement.

Having done all my APL on these IBM systems, I have no direct experience of the joys of □FMT, □VR, etc., or of the concept of 'component files' which the bureaux have pioneered. The formatting function is one which catches me very much in two minds: on the one hand it strays a long way (both in form and purpose) from the original purity and consistency of APL; on the other hand it does provide professional programmers with the kind of tool they expect to find in a commercial environment. Never having had □FMT, I personally don't miss it, but I'm sure there must be very many ex-bureau systems which have acquired hastily-written ΔFMT functions to cover a move in-house. To all these people (and those anticipating such a move) I apologise – there is no ΔFMT to be found here, because I have never seen a good one. It's the kind of task that just doesn't seem to square with APL's philosophical base, which is probably why IBM haven't given us a □FMT in the first place. Until they do, my advice to bureau users would be to use □FMT where it is necessary, not where it is convenient. Otherwise they may find themselves tied much more firmly to the bureau than they had anticipated!

The second major contribution which the bureaux have made to 'commercial APL' is the idea of component files, and here the VS APL user can follow, albeit slightly clumsily.

This is another area where there would be little point in my giving detailed code, because the shared variables of VS APL are used very differently in the assorted environments. For example under CMS you can safely use files of APL objects written and read without conversion; under VSPC such files are available but are much less convenient, and waste a great deal of space. What I think you should do is to bury all file access under cover functions which follow the principles of the 'component file' system. Not only does this make the code more readable at the application level, but it also insulates you from a change of environment, and ensures that the file access is done as efficiently as possible. The typical form of these cover functions is

```
RC←   .. filename ..   FUNCTION   .. variables ..
```

or

```
RC←FUNCTION   .. filename
```

If you follow the naming conventions established by the bureaux,

```
→(RC←ΔFCREATE 'MYFILE')↑FAIL
```

or

```
→(RC←'MYFILE' ΔAPPEND 'ΔDATA')↑FAIL
```

etc.

Two additional functions which I find useful are

```
RC←'MYFILE' ΔDUMP 'ΔDATA ΔDESCR ΔTABLE'
```

and

```
RC←'MYFILE' ΔGET 'ΔTABLE ΔDATA'

RC←'MYFILE' ΔGET ' '
```

The first of these creates (or overwrites) the file 'MYFILE' with all the variables given in the list. The second retrieves either selected variables or the entire contents of the file. These functions are particularly useful where you have a system broken down into several workspaces, which pass information to one another in the form of APL variables. If you can design a batch program to take conventionally structured data, and invert it to the same format as your component files, then you have a very powerful tool indeed for data enquiry.

File access is a subject where the 'tricks of the trade' depend heavily on the way your particular APL has been set up, and I can't really offer any more constructive advice here. I now want to move on to look at three topics, all relevant to the aim of making life easier for the APL programmer: (a) a decent editor for functions and variables; (b) a design and editing system for full-screen panels; (c) functions to automate workspace documentation. The first two of these are aimed specifically at screen-based systems, the third is more generally applicable.

Full-screen Editing for Functions and Variables

Even on a teletype the ∇ editor always struck me as being somewhat feeble-minded; on a VDU it is utterly inadequate, and should have been replaced long ago. Rumour has it that the next release of VS APL does have considerably better editing, but I still think it worthwhile to run through the main characteristics of a good screen-based function-editor. It is interesting to note that a function to achieve these breaks virtually every convention in Chapter 5! My version is called 'Δ': it is (at the last count) 171 statements long, branches to line numbers, is totally uncommented, and uses distinctly non-mnemonic three-character local names. For a function like this, the criteria on which the code is judged are very different from the usual: it must be compact, efficient, economical in its use of symbols, and easily copied and erased. By creating a 171-statement megalith you achieve all of these; in fact 'Δ' makes only 28 symbol-table entries, and occupies just under 10K of workspace. Of course there is a parallel version which is commented and branches to labels, and this is the one that gets amended, before being stripped down to the production version. Enough, anyway, of this digression. What should a reasonable full-screen editor do, and how should you set about writing one? Oddly enough, the first half of the problem is very much the hardest part – the actual coding is tedious rather than difficult. Obviously the design of my editor has evolved over a long period, and it is still averaging one change every couple of months or so. As I write, its functional specification goes like this:

- It will edit functions (as long as they are not suspended) and character matrices, up to 135 characters wide, and up to 500 lines long.

- You can move from function to function, function to variable, etc., without leaving Edit. When leaving an object you can either 'SAVE' and preserve the changes you have made, or 'QUIT' to leave it as it was.

- The size of the screen window is 20 lines by 71 columns, and can be scrolled horizontally and vertically (Up, Scroll, →, ←).

- On this window, you can overtype any line, or add new lines up to 12 at a time (see Insert); erase a line, by pressing 'ERASE EOF' at the start of it (functions only); restore the window (CLEAR); put it back into the fn/var, and return the cursor to the command area (ENTER).

So far, this is all easy stuff, and it covers 95% of the actual use of 'Δ'. However, there are some operations which can't easily be done in full-screen mode (e.g. Move, or the replacement of one string with another throughout a function), so in the true spirit of Pareto's law, the remaining 95% of 'Δ' only does about 5% of the work! In fact the reason it has such a full range of editing commands is largely historical; it was originally written under CMS before we had AP 124 and I wanted to make it look as similar to the CMS editor as I could. The command area of the screen is 50 characters long, and will accept any stack (separated by commas) of commands. In case of any unrecognizable (or impossible!) command, the culprit is displayed in a highlighted field, and the rest of the stack is cancelled. Most of the commands only need an initial letter (e.g. 'T' will do for 'TOP'), so here they are, with a note on the amount of code needed to do each one:

Command	Example	Lines of APL	Result
p	12	2	Centres window on line 12, and puts the cursor there
T, B, S, U, N	N5	One each	Moves window around vertically
Locate	L E̲X̲I̲T̲	4	Finds next occurrence of 'E̲X̲I̲T̲'
Insert p	I5	6	Leaves 12 blank lines after line 5, and puts the cursor on the new line 6
Ip text	I6 COMMENT	4	COMMENT becomes line 7
DELete p/n	DEL 5/6	9	Removes lines 5 and 6
Move p/n	M 4/7	10	Lines 4–7 are moved to follow the line currently in the middle of the window
Alter Replace	A FRED/JOE 1/99 R IN OUT 5	26	Replacement of character string. 'Alter' does this regardless of context; 'replace' only changes valid APL names, i.e. it won't touch 'IN' in the middle of 'PRINT'
Get object	G EDIT 5/6 G5	15	Lines 5 and 6 of 'EDIT' are included after the current line Line 5 of the function being edited is included after the current line, i.e. it is duplicated
Width n	W90	4	Changes function width, e.g. to allow a longer header to be typed in
Width	W	1	Displays current width
STAck char	STA!	2	Temporarily makes '!' the stack delimiter

Because of its 'current line' heritage, '∆' still maintains a pointer to the centre line of the window, and shows this with an arrow at the side of the function. All the commands assume 'current line only' as the default, e.g. 'DEL' just deletes the arrowed line; 'I COMMENT' would make the next line 'COMMENT', etc. Because '∆' always moves the arrow to the line where you left the cursor, you can do commands like 'Move' very easily, by typing the command, putting the cursor on the destination line, and pressing 'Enter'.

I would say the biggest drawback of this editor is its inability to execute lines of code whilst editing the function in which they occur. You can get round this by trying out the line, putting quotes round it, assigning it into a character variable, opening Edit, and 'Getting' it, but this is a decidedly laborious process. One final feature is the use of the commands 'X', 'Y', and 'Z' to store any string of other commands. Typically you might want to change 'DATA' to 'ΔDATA' in half a dozen functions, in which case the command

    'X R DATA ΔDATA 0/99, SAVE'

means you only have to type

    'X, ΔNEXTFN'

do stack, and move Edit to 'NEXTFN' - to make each change.
    When you close Edit (Quit or FILE), it returns:

'EDIT CLOSED'	for Quit
'EDIT CLOSED: FUNCTION < FRED > FIXED'	for FILE

This leads to code like

```
      NEW←EDΔMAT OLD;TEMP
      --------------------

[1]   ⍝EDIT NUMERIC MATRIX

[2]   NEW←OLD
[3]   TEMP← 6 0 DFMT OLD
[4]   →(12=ρΔ 'TEMP')↑0
[5]   NEW←(ρOLD)↑ΔMATEXEC TEMP
    ∇
```

for a distinctly quick and dirty (but quite effective) numeric edit.
    I am obviously not going to irritate you with 170 statements of terse and incomprehensible code; however, just for interest, here are statements 90-99 which do the 'MOVE' command:

```
[90]   CMD←(~∧\CMD∈'MOVE ')/CMD
[91]   →((∧/CMD∈NUM,'/: ')×ρCMD)↓WHAT
[92]   CMD[(CMD∈'/:')/⍳ρCMD]←' '
[93]   CMD←0⌈(1↑ρΔΔF)⌊1+2ρ±CMD
[94]   F←ΔΔF[CMD←CMD[1],CMD[1]+⍳0⌈--/CMD;]
[95]   ΔΔF←(~(⍳1↑ρΔΔF)∈CMD)/ΔΔF
[96]   ΔΔP←0⌈(1+1↑ρΔΔF)⌊ΔΔP-(ρCMD)×CMD[1]<ΔΔP
[97]   ΔΔF←(~(⍳(1↑ρΔΔF)+1↑ρF)∈ΔΔP+⍳1↑ρF)\ΔΔF
[98]   ΔΔF[ΔΔP+⍳1↑ρF;]←F
[99]   →CONTINUE,ΔΔP←(1↑ρΔΔF)⌊ΔΔP+1↑ρF
```

ΔΔF is the □CR of the function being edited; ΔΔP is the current line pointer; CMD looks like 'MO 2/5', say; NUM is just '0123456789'.
    After lines 90-93, CMD has been validated, and interpreted to '2 5'. Line 94 turns this into '2 3 4 5', and takes a copy (called F) of these lines of ΔΔF. Notice the implicit validation, which deals with

M5	line 5 only

or

M7/3	line 7 only, rather than falling over!

Line 95 chops out the moved lines, and line 96 adjusts the pointer to compensate. Lines 97 and 98 open a suitable gap, and drop in the saved lines, and line 99 resets the pointer to the end of the moved chunk. It really is all easy stuff, just rather tedious, and you certainly ought to hire a tame idiot for a day or two to test it. 'Δ' now falls over very rarely indeed, but I'm sure it could still be beaten by a really determined assailant with a sufficiently warped mind!

Full-screen Panel Design and Editing

You will remember from Chapter 9 that the screen is split into a number of fields

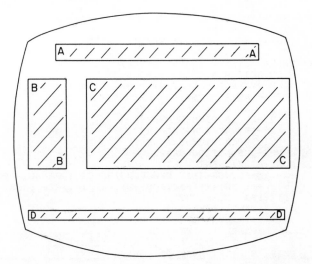

which are defined by a six-column matrix, with one row for each field:

	Location		Shape		Att	Int
Field *A*	2	5	3	50	2	1
Field *B*	6	2	10	5	2	2
Field *C*	6	10	10	60	0	1
Field *D*	24	2	1	78	2	1

With only four fields to consider, we could just about get by with

```
FSMΔFMT 4 6ρ 2 5 3 50 2 1, ... etc.
```

but for more complex screens some form of mechanization is obviously highly desirable.

This mechanization seems to break down naturally into four phases (five if you want labelled fields) which are as follows: (a) defining the fields in the first place;

```
      DRAW STK;PANEL;ΔFMT;ΔTEXT;ACTION;POS
      ------------------------------------
[1]           ⍝USE FULL-SCREEN FACILITIES TO DRAW/AMEND PANELS,
[2]           ⍝AND SEE THE RESULTS BEFORE YOUR VERY EYES.

[3]           →(1=0=1↑0⍴PANEL←(¯1+POS←⌊/STKι' ',/')↑STK←,STK)↑CANT
[4]           →(NEW,CANT,OLD,CANT,CANT)[1+⎕NC PANEL]
[5]      CANT:→0,⍴⎕←'NAME <<',(▼PANEL),'>> IS NOT AVAILABLE'
[6]       NEW:→CONT,⍴ΔFMT← 0 7 ⍴0
[7]       OLD:ΔFMT←(¯2↑ 1 1 ,⍴ΔFMT)⍴ΔFMT←≖PANEL
[8]           →(PR,INT,TXT,CONT)[¯3+1↓⍴ΔFMT]
[9]        PR:ΔFMT←ΔFMT,2
[10]      INT:ΔFMT←ΔFMT,1
[11]      TXT:ΔFMT←ΔFMT,0
[12]     CONT:→(×⎕NC PANEL,'ΔTEXT')↑SETTEXT
[13]          →ST,⍴ΔTEXT←' '
[14] SETTEXT:≖'ΔTEXT←',PANEL,'ΔTEXT'
[15]       ST:ACTION←5|'1234'ι1↑POS↓STK
[16]      LKP:→(MEN,DR,CH,AT,TT,DONE,HP)[0 1 2 3 4 12 ιACTION]
[17]      MEN:→LKP,ACTION←DRAWΔMENU PANEL
[18]       DR:→LKP,ACTION←DRAWΔINP
[19]       CH:→LKP,ACTION←DRAWΔCHK
[20]       AT:→LKP,ACTION←DRAWΔATT
[21]       TT:→LKP,ACTION←DRAWΔTXT
[22]       HP:→LKP,ACTION←DRAWΔHLP
[23]     DONE:→(××/⍴ΔFMT)↓SKIP
[24]          ⎕←ACTION←'FIX NEW VERSION OF ',PANEL,' ? :- '
[25]          →(('YN'=1↑(⍴ACTION)↓⎕),1)/FIX,SKIP,DONE
[26]      FIX:≖PANEL,'←ΔFMT'
[27]          'PANEL FIXED'
[28]          →(∨/×ΔFMT[;7])↓SKIP
[29]          ≖PANEL,'ΔTEXT←ΔTEXT'
[30]          'TEXT SAVED AS ',PANEL,'ΔTEXT'
[31]     SKIP:'END OF PANEL DESIGN'
[32]          FSMΔCLOSE
      ∇
```

Figure 10.1

(b) checking the fields, and moving/extending/deleting them as necessary; (c) setting the attributes and intensities; (d) entering permanent text, such as headings, or underscore fillers for input fields. Each of these will occupy the whole screen, so there is no room for a command area, or any helpful messages. This places two constraints on the dialogue:

- It must be entirely PF key driven.
- It must be almost childishly simple to use.

With these in mind, I want first to look at the calling function, and then in detail at each of the four sub-sections; the code is a good illustration of the programming structures which I mentioned in Chapter 4.

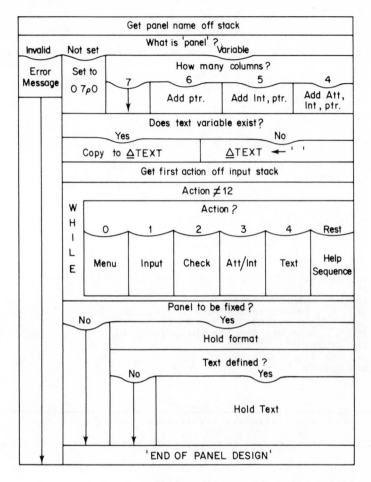

Figure 10.1

We start with the main routine, called DRAW. See Figure 10.1

This starts by checking for a valid format name, and picks up the associated text, if any. It then offers a menu of options (PF keys 1–4, PF12 to close, and anything else for 'help'), and branches to the appropriate sub-section. Each of these is terminated by either 'Enter' – in which case it returns zero – or a PF key. By this means DRAW can be driven between any of the four phases (or to the exit) without returning to the menu in between. The design process is closed with PF key 12, and DRAW checks that you really do want to overwrite the old panel definition before it does so. If no permanent text has been defined, it doesn't bother to save a text vector.

So to the first phase of panel design proper: DRAWΔINP (Figure 10.2).

All that is achieved by lines 3–9 in Figure 10.2 is a pretty screen layout, on which row or column numbers are clearly marked:

```
     ACTION←DRAWΔINP;FRAME;LAB;CT;FM;POS
     -----------------------------------

[1]        ⍝ALLOW PANELS TO BE DRAWN/REDRAWN ON THE SCREEN.

[2]        FSMΔFMT 1 1 24 79 0
[3]        FRAME← 24 79 ρ'.'
[4]        FRAME[;1+10×⍳7]←'|'
[5]        FRAME[10 20 ;]←'-'
[6]        FRAME[5 10 15 20 ;1+10×⍳7]←'+'
[7]        FRAME[1 2 ;1+10×⍳7]←'1234567',[0.5] '1'
[8]        FRAME[;⍳2]←(24↑9ρ1)⌽ 24 2 ρ 2 0 ⍕⍳24
[9]        FRAME←,FRAME
[10]       →LAB←((1↑ρΔFMT)ρLOOP1),WRITE,CT←1
[11] LOOP1:→(0∊ΔFMT[CT;⍳4])↑SKIP1
[12]       POS←ΔFMT[CT; 1 2],[1.5] ‾1++/ 2 2 ρΔFMT[CT;]
[13]       FRAME[1+ 24 79 ⊥POS-1]←□AV[65+CT]
[14] SKIP1:→LAB[CT←CT+1]
[15] WRITE:1 FSMΔW FRAME
[16]       ACTION←FSMΔPF
[17]       →(' '∧.=FRAME←,FSMΔR 1)↑DONE
[18]       FM←((+/V\⌽□AV[65+⍳53]∊FRAME),7)ρ0
[19]       →LAB←((1↑ρFM)ρLOOP),EXIT,CT←1
[20]  LOOP:→(ρPOS←(FRAME=□AV[65+CT])/⍳1896)↓SKIP2
[21]       POS←(0,0<-/POS[2;])⌽POS←1+ 24 79 ⊤‾1+2ρPOS
[22]       FM[CT;]←(4↑POS[;1],1+--/POS), 2 1 0
[23]       →(CT>1↑ρΔFMT)↑SKIP2
[24]       →(0∊ΔFMT[CT;⍳4])↑SKIP2
[25]       FM[CT; 5 6 7]←ΔFMT[CT; 5 6 7]
[26] SKIP2:→LAB[CT←CT+1]
[27] EXIT:ΔFMT←FM
[28] DONE:
     ∇
```

Figure 10.2

```
*********************************
*1  ........1.........2.........3..
*2  ........1.........1.........1..
*3  ........|.........|.........|..
*4  ........|.........|.........|..
*5  ........+.........+.........+..
*6  ........|.........|.........|..
*7  ........|.........|.........|..
*8  ........|.........|.........|..
*9  ........|.........|.........|..
*10--------+---------+---------+--
*
```

Lines 10-14 whip round drawing in any existing fields, by marking two corners
with the letters A-Z, Δ, and A-Z (i.e. □AV[65+ ⍳ 53]). The screen is then held,
the user's action recorded, and the whole lot is read back in again.

```
*********************************
*1  ........1.........2.........3..
*2  ........1.........1.........1..
*3  ........|.........|.........|..
*4  ........A.........|..B......|..
*5  ........+.........+.........+..
*6  ........|.........A.........|..
*7  ........|.........|..B...|..
*8  ........|.........|.........|..
*9  ........|.........|.........|..
*10--------+---------+---------+--
*
```

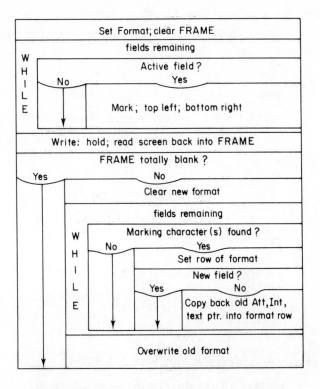

Figure 10.2

Each pair of letters defines a field (a single letter is treated as a pair in the same place), and is turned into a row in the new format matrix by lines 21 and 22. If the field existed already, then its old attribute, intensity, and text pointer are copied back (line 25), otherwise the field is given the default of output/normal/no text.

Suppose we marked the 'PF1' screen with a couple of 'As', then pressed PF2:

This is the second phase of screen-design, in which fields may be moved, extended, or deleted. It also shows any overlapping fields with dominoes in the area of overlap, and indicates obscured areas with quads:

```
      ACTION←DRAWΔCHK;FRAME;LAB;CT;ROW;COL;MULT;CH
      ------------------------------------------------
[1]        ⍝CHECK CURRENT FMT: UPDATES ΔFMT FROM ROOT FN.
[2]        FSMΔFMT 1 1 24 79 0
[3]        FRAME← 24 79 ⍴65
[4]        →LAB←((1↑⍴ΔFMT)⍴LOOP),WR,CT←1
[5]   LOOP:→(0∈ΔFMT[CT;⍳4])↑SKIP
[6]        ROW←¯1+ΔFMT[CT;1]+⍳0⌈ΔFMT[CT;3]
[7]        COL←¯1+ΔFMT[CT;2]+⍳0⌈ΔFMT[CT;4]
[8]        FRAME[ROW;COL]←(179,CT+65)[1+FRAME[ROW;COL]=65]
[9]        →(COL←¯1+1↑COL)↓SKIP
[10]       FRAME[ROW;COL]← 159 188[1+FRAME[ROW;COL]>65]
[11]  SKIP:→LAB[CT←CT+1]
[12]    WR:1 FSMΔW ⎕AV[FRAME]
[13]       ACTION←FSMΔPF
[14]       FRAME←FSMΔR 1
[15]       →LAB←((1↑⍴ΔFMT)⍴LP2),DONE,CT←1
[16]   LP2:→(0∈ΔFMT[CT;⍳4])↑UND
[17]       ROW←24⌊¯1+ΔFMT[CT;1]+⍳0⌈ΔFMT[CT;3]
[18]       COL←79⌊¯1+ΔFMT[CT;2]+⍳0⌈ΔFMT[CT;4]
[19]       CH←,FRAME[ROW;COL]
[20]       →(CT DRAWΔCHΔEXT CH)↑DEL
[21]       →((⍴CH)<⌊/CH⍳'↑↓←→')↑DEL
[22]       MULT←10⌊⌊/'123456789I'⍳CH
[23]       ΔFMT[CT;2]←(80-ΔFMT[CT;4])⌊1⌈ΔFMT[CT;2]+MULT×-/'→←'∊CH
[24]       ΔFMT[CT;1]←(25-ΔFMT[CT;3])⌊1⌈ΔFMT[CT;1]+MULT×-/'↓↑'∊CH
[25]   DEL:ΔFMT[CT;]←ΔFMT[CT;]×~'∇'∊CH
[26]   UND:→LAB[CT←CT+1]
[27]  DONE:
      ∇
```

```
      RC←CT DRAWΔCHΔEXT CH;OLD;MULT;TAB;TEXT
      -----------------------------------------
[1]        ⍝EXTEND (OR CHOP) FIELD IN ANY DIRECTION.
[2]        ⍝<<CH>> IS THE RAVELLED CHARACTERS FROM FIELD <<CT>>
[3]        ⍝UPDATES ΔFMT AND ΔTEXT FROM ROOT FN

[4]        →(∨/'-+'∊CH)↓RC←0
[5]        TAB← 4 4 ⍴ ¯1 0 1 0 0 0 1 0 0 ¯1 0 1 0 0 0 1
[6]        MULT←(¯1*'-'∊CH)×10|⌊/'1234567890'⍳CH
[7]        OLD←ΔFMT[CT; 3 4]
[8]        ΔFMT[CT;⍳4]←ΔFMT[CT;⍳4]+MULT×TAB[4⌊⌊/'↑↓←→'⍳CH;]
[9]        ΔFMT[CT;⍳4]← 1 1 0 0 ⌈ 24 79 24 79 ⌊ΔFMT[CT;⍳4]
[10]       ΔFMT[CT;⍳4]←((25 80 -ΔFMT[CT; 3 4]), 24 79)⌊ΔFMT[CT;⍳4]

[11]       ⍝PAD TEXT (IF ANY) AS REQUIRED

[12]       →ΔFMT[CT;7]↓DONE
[13]       TEXT←ΔTEXT[POS←(⍴ΔTEXT)⌊ΔFMT[CT;7]+⍳×/OLD]
[14]       ΔFMT[;7]←ΔFMT[;7]-(×/OLD)×ΔFMT[;7]≥ΔFMT[CT;7]
[15]       ΔFMT[CT;7]←⍴ΔTEXT←(~(⍳⍴ΔTEXT)∊POS)/ΔTEXT
[16]       ΔTEXT←ΔTEXT,,(ΔFMT[CT; 3 4])↑OLD⍴TEXT
[17]  DONE:RC←1
      ∇
```

Figure 10.3

```
***********************************
*
*
*
*        <AAAAAAAAAAAAAAA
*        <AAAAAAAAAA▦▦▦BBBBB
*        <AAAAAAAAAA▦▦▦BBBBB
*                    <BBBBBBBB
*
*
*
```

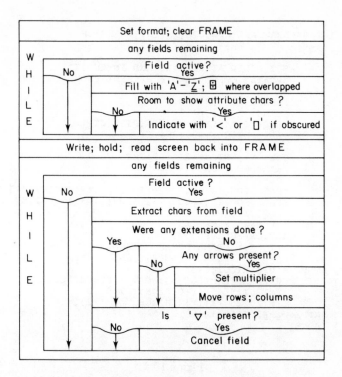

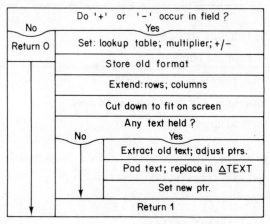

Figure 10.3

Thus making potential disasters pretty obvious! This is handled by statements 2-12 of DRAW△CHK (Figure 10.3), which incidentally breaks one of my rules (Chapter 5) by indexing □AV explicitly to get '⊞□<'.

Having set up the screen, it holds it, reads it back, and takes each field in turn to check for possible changes. The sort of thing it accepts is:

122

```
ACTION←DRAWΔATT;ROW;COL;LAB;CT;FRAME;CH
----------------------------------------
[1]        ⍝SET FIELD ATTRIBUTES AND INTENSITIES.
[2]        ⍝UPDATES COLS 5 AND 6 OF ΔFMT FROM ROOT FN.

[3]        FSMΔFMT 1 1 24 79 0
[4]        FRAME← 24 79 ⍴' '
[5]       →LAB←((1↑⍴ΔFMT)⍴LOOP1),DISP,CT←1
[6]  LOOP1:→(0∊ΔFMT[CT;⍳4])↑SKIP
[7]        ROW←¯1+ΔFMT[CT;1]+⍳0⌈ΔFMT[CT;3]
[8]        COL←¯1+ΔFMT[CT;2]+⍳0⌈ΔFMT[CT;4]
[9]        FRAME[ROW;COL]←'+'
[10]       COL←78⌊COL
[11]       FRAME[ROW[1];COL[1]]←'IO'[1⌈2⌊1+ΔFMT[CT;5]]
[12]       FRAME[ROW[1];1+COL[1]]←'ZNH'[1⌈3⌊1+ΔFMT[CT;6]]
[13]  SKIP:→LAB[CT←CT+1]
[14]  DISP:1 FSMΔW FRAME
[15]       ACTION←FSMΔPF
[16]       →(' '∧.=,FRAME←FSMΔR 1)↑DONE
[17]       →LAB←((1↑⍴ΔFMT)⍴LOOP2),DONE,CT←1
[18] LOOP2:→(0∊ΔFMT[CT;⍳4])↑SKIP2
[19]       CH←FRAME[ΔFMT[CT;1]; 0 1 +78⌊ΔFMT[CT;2]]
[20]       ΔFMT[CT;5]←1↑((('OI'∊CH)/ 2 0),2
[21]       ΔFMT[CT;6]←1↑((('ZNH'∊CH)/ 0 1 2),1
[22] SKIP2:→LAB[CT←CT+1]
[23]  DONE:
      ∇
```

Figure 10.4

→	move field one place right
↑5	move field five places up
+2↓	add two rows to bottom of field
-3	remove three right-most columns of field
∇	delete field altogether

All of these may be typed anywhere in the field, e.g. the screen shown as

```
**********************************
*
*
*
*         <AAAAAAAAAAAAAAA
*         <AAAAA↓2AAAAAAAA
*         <AAAAAAAAAAAAAAA
*
*
```

will move field *A* down two rows. Again, most of the validation is implicit, such as the check on lines 21 and 22 to make sure you don't move any fields clean off the screen!

Field extension is handled by a separate function, DRAWΔCHΔEXT, which is called once for every screen field checked. Line 2 sends it straight out if it can't

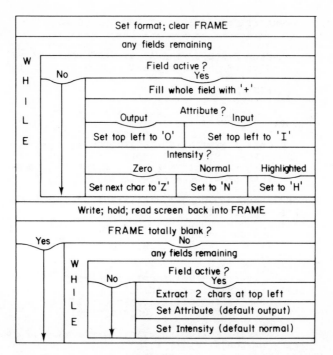

Figure 10.4

find a '+' or a '−', otherwise it checks for 'above or below', and decides how many extra rows/columns are needed (the default is one column to the right). Having amended the format matrix, it proceeds to pad (or chop) any fixed text to match. Finally it returns 1 to stop 'move' getting confused by all those arrows!

Setting attributes and intensities is by far the most straightforward section of panel design, and the structure of 'DRAWΔATT' is very similar to the two functions we have just seen (see Figure 10.4).

Possible attributes are 'O' for output and 'I' for input; possible intensities are 'Z' for zero (hidden), 'N' for normal, and 'H' for highlighted. The defaults are set when the fields are first defined, and such a field would look like

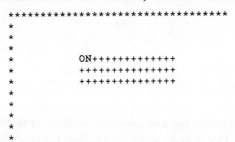

It could then be changed (e.g. to input highlighted) by overtyping the top left-hand corner with the appropriate letters ('IH' in this case).

```
       ACTION←DRAWΔTXT;FRAME;LAB;CT;ROW;COL;CH;POS
       ---------------------------------------------
[1]           ⍝HOLD FIXED TEXT AGAINST PANEL DEFINITION
[2]           ⍝UPDATES ΔFMT AND ΔTEXT FROM ROOT FUNCTION.

[3]           FSMΔFMT 1 1 24 79 0
[4]           FRAME← 24 79 ρ' '
[5]           →LAB←((1↑ρΔFMT)ρLOOP),EXIT,CT←1
[6]     LOOP:→(0∈ΔFMT[CT;⍳4])↑SKIP
[7]           ROW←⁻1+ΔFMT[CT;1]+⍳0⌈ΔFMT[CT;3]
[8]           COL←⁻1+ΔFMT[CT;2]+⍳0⌈ΔFMT[CT;4]
[9]           →(POS←ΔFMT[CT;7])↓UNDEF
[10]          CH←ΔTEXT[(ρΔTEXT)⌊,POS+⍳×/ΔFMT[CT; 3 4]]
[11]          FRAME[ROW;COL]←ΔFMT[CT; 3 4]ρCH
[12]          →SKIP
[13]    UNDEF:FRAME[ROW;COL]←'⍳∘'[1+×ΔFMT[CT;5]]
[14]     SKIP:→LAB[CT←CT+1]
[15]     EXIT:1 FSMΔW FRAME
[16]          ACTION←FSMΔPF
[17]          →(' '∧.=,FRAME←FSMΔR 1)↑DONE
[18]          ΔTEXT←1ρ' '
[19]          ΔFMT[;7]←0
[20]          →LAB←((1↑ρΔFMT)ρLOOP2),DONE,CT←1
[21]    LOOP2:→(0∈ΔFMT[CT;⍳4])↑SKIP2
[22]          ROW←⁻1+ΔFMT[CT;1]+⍳0⌈ΔFMT[CT;3]
[23]          COL←⁻1+ΔFMT[CT;2]+⍳0⌈ΔFMT[CT;4]
[24]          CH←,FRAME[ROW;COL]
[25]          →(SKIP2,SCAL,HOLDTXT)[1+(~'∇'∈CH)×2⌊+/~CH∈'⍳∘']
[26]     SCAL:CH←(ρCH)ρ(~CH∈'⍳∘')/CH
[27]  HOLDTXT:CH[(CH∈'⍳∘')/⍳ρCH]←' '
[28]          ΔFMT[CT;7]←ρΔTEXT
[29]          ΔTEXT←ΔTEXT,CH
[30]    SKIP2:→LAB[CT←CT+1]
[31]     DONE:
      ∇
```

Figure 10.5

That leaves only the fixing of text into permanent fields, such as headings and 'help' messages (Figure 10.5). Any fields as yet without text are filled up with iotas and jots for input and output fields respectively; otherwise the previously entered text is displayed. The text is then reassigned field by field (lines 19–28), the one refinement being that if only one character is entered in a field, it is replicated to fill the entire field:

```
******************          ********************
*                           *
*                           *
*  o o o o o o o o o         *
*  oA o TITLE o     o_ o o   ------->>  *  A TITLE     ____
*  o o o o o o o o o   o o o o           *             ____
*                           *
```

A '∇' anywhere in a field will cancel all the text previously entered for that field, and an additional possibility (not shown here) would be to allow the text for any field to be edited as if it were a character matrix, i.e. to call the full-screen editor from within 'DRAW'.

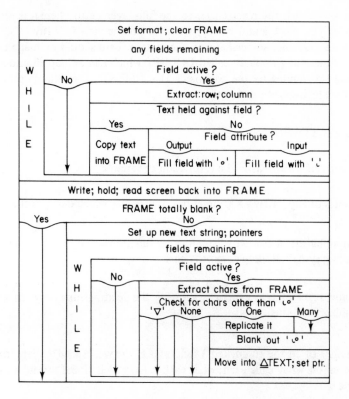

Figure 10.5

That is all I want to say on the subject of high-level panel design. Used in conjunction with the FSM functions of Chapter 9 it is a remarkably flexible and powerful tool; what's more it really is fun to use! Being able to type '→3' or '↑4' into a succession of fields, press PF2, and watch them leap to their appointed places is a positively exhilarating experience. I hope you find this too, but even if you don't use my panel-design method as it stands, then I trust that these examples of properly structured, clearly coded APL will still help when you come to write similar software yourself.

Automatic Documentation

This must be the dream of anyone who has ever programmed a computer! Well, in Chapter 7 I said it was possible, so I had better set about proving it. The twin aims of any system documentation are (a) to make 'fire-fighting' as simple as possible; (b) to allow easy change in the future – not necessarily by the system author. Armed only with □NL and □CR, the determined APL programmer can go a long way towards satisfying these needs, but for once it isn't a particularly easy task. In fact it is very much the reverse case to the full-screen editor; here it is very easy to define what you want, and decidedly tricky to program it efficiently.

First the easy bit: somewhere on the system there should be made available a group of functions (probably called DOCGP), which can be copied into any workspace, and set running by the command 'DOCUMENT'. They should produce (preferably on a high-speed printer) the following:

- date and time (on every page)

- a copy of 'DESCRIBE', be it function or variable

- copies of any 'HOWXXX' functions or variables which occur in the workspace

- an alphabetical contents list, showing function name; number of statements; calling syntax; leading comment lines

- some form of tree-structure, showing the relationships between called and calling functions

- listings of all the (unlocked!) functions in the workspace (except itself), with notes on what calls each; what each calls; which global variables each references

- a pictorial representation of all the full-screen panels, showing the text held against each

- an alphabetical list of all global variables, showing type; shape; where referenced

The problem lies in how one sets about producing these for a reasonably large workspace, without chewing up a quite absurd amount of CPU. The best I can offer is between 20 and 50s of CPU time (IBM 3032) to run a full documentation on what I consider to be a reasonably big workspace (1000–2000 statements; upwards of 100 functions). I know this sounds a lot, but set against the time taken to compile a 500-statement PL/1 program (typically 40–50 s) it isn't really too terrible. If you can find some way of running your DOCUMENTs overnight in batch, then so much the better; if not there are still some 400 min in the working day, and you have as much right to one of these as your PL/1 colleagues!

The overall structure of 'DOCUMENT' looks rather like this:

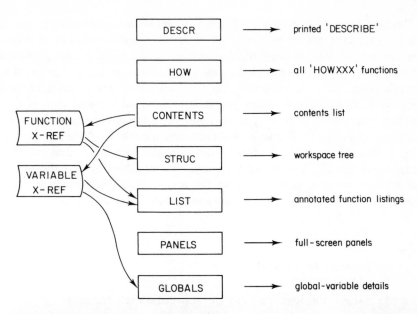

The first subject I want to consider in detail is the creation of those function and variable cross-reference tables. Once these exist, the rest of the job is relatively plain sailing, although the structure analysis is worth a paragraph or two - if only as an interesting example of the use of recursion! The object is to end up with a two-column matrix of indices into the tables of names, the first column being the calling function, the second the function it calls:

ROOT	ROOTΔFN1
ROOT	ROOTΔFN2
ROOTΔFN2	UTIL1
ROOTΔFN2	UTIL2
.	.
.	.
.	.

Calling   *Called*

- and similarly for functions and referenced variables.

128

Clearly we must take the □CR of each function in turn, and having printed its details on the contents list we must then check it for any functions which it mentions, or any variables it refers to. The way *not* to do this is to take each other function name in turn, and perform a string-search for that name. For one thing this tells you far more than you really need to know, and in a well structured workspace with lots of small functions you have just created a nested loop of CPU-gobbling proportions. A far better, but somewhat more subtle approach is to cut down your function to a table of the names which *might* be global. It then only takes a single '∧.=' against the lists of functions and variables to sieve out those names which need to be appended to each of your tables. Here is the code to reduce any function to such a list of names: it is worth quoting if only as a quite remarkable selection of the more obscure idioms from Chapter 8!

```
     OCC←ΔSTRIP FN;HEADER;ALPH
     -------------------------

[1]  ⍝CHOP FN DOWN TO LIST OF NON-LOCALISED NAMES.

[2]    ALPH←'1234567890',□AV[65+⍳54]
[3]    FN←□CR FN

[4]  ⍝FIRST SET UP HEADER AS CHECKLIST.

[5]    HEADER←' ;←' ΔTAB FN[1;]
[6]    FN← 1 0 ↓FN

[7]  ⍝CHOP OUT COMMENT LINES, AND RAVEL:

[8]    FN←,((~FN∨.='⍝')/FN),' '

[9]  ⍝THEN SCRAP ANYTHING WITHIN QUOTES:

[10]   FN←(~(FN='''')∨≠\FN='''')/FN

[11] ⍝SUBSTITUTE BLANK FOR NON-ALPH AND CHOP MULT BLANKS:

[12]   FN[(~FN∈ALPH)/⍳⍴FN]←' '
[13]   FN←(~(' '=FN)∧' '=1⌽FN)/FN

[14] ⍝SET UP REMAINING NAMES AS TABLE:

[15]   FN←' ' ΔTAB FN

[16] ⍝CHOP OUT ROWS WHICH ARE ALL NUMERIC:

[17]   FN←(~∧/FN∈' 0123456789')/FN

[18] ⍝REMOVE NAMES REFERENCED IN HEADER:

[19]   FN←(~∨/FN∧.=⍉((1↑⍴HEADER),1↓⍴FN)↑HEADER)/FN

[20] ⍝FINALLY TAKE OUT DUPLICATES:

[21]   OCC←(1 1 ⍉<\FN∧.=⍉FN)/FN
     ∇
```

You may recall from Chapter 4 that there are two main criteria which determine whether a problem should be defined recursively: (a) it should decompose into sub-problems which are either trivial, or break down in the same way as the main problem; (b) at some stage it must back-track either to the main problem, or to a previous sub-problem.

The task of drawing out a structure-tree from the function cross-reference table is just such a problem, and illustrates the use of recursion very well.

ROOT . . .

   : ROOTΔFN1

   : ROOTΔFN2 . . .

       :UTIL1

       :UTIL2

   : ROOTΔFN3

       : . . . , etc.

Here the main problem is to draw the structure of ROOT. The first sub-problem (to draw ROOTΔFN1) is trivial; the second is to draw ROOTΔFN2. This goes down one level further to two trivial sub-sub-problems, and then back-tracks to attack ROOTΔFN3 and so on. Figure 10.6 illustrates the functions to do it.

```
        NAMELIST ΔSTRUC XREF;LEN;ROOTS;PAGE;NEST
        -----------------------------------------

[1]        ⍝DRAW OUT WS STRUCTURE AS TREE
[2]        ⍝    NAMELIST IS A CHARACTER TABLE OF FN NAMES.
[3]        ⍝    XREF IS A TWO-COLUMN MATRIX OF CLNG/CLD PTRS.
[4]        ⍝TAKE SIMPLEST ROOTS FIRST

[5]        ROOTS←(~(⍳1↑⍴NAMELIST)∊XREF[;2])/⍳1↑⍴NAMELIST
[6]        ROOTS←ROOTS[⍋+/ROOTS∘.=XREF[;1]]

[7]        ⍝RUN THROUGH EACH ROOT IN TURN

[8]        ROOTS←0,ROOTS
[9]  LOOP:→(⍴ROOTS←1↓ROOTS)↓DONE
[10]       NEST←PAGE←⍳0
[11]       0 ΔTREE ROOTS[1]

[12]       ⍝DISPLAY COMPLETED PAGE, SUITABLY INDENTED

[13]       LEN←10⌈2+1↑⍴NAMELIST
[14]       0 1 ↓(-LEN×NEST)⌽((⍴NEST),80)↑':',NAMELIST[PAGE;]
[15]       →LOOP
[16] DONE:'WS STRUCTURE ANALYSIS COMPLETE'
        ∇


        LEVEL ΔTREE FROM;TO
        -------------------

[1]        ⍝RECURSIVE TREE SEARCH ...
[2]        ⍝UPDATES <<NEST>> AND <<PAGE>> FROM ΔSTRUC.

[3]        →(⍴TO←(FROM=XREF[;1])/XREF[;2])↑MORE

[4]        ⍝WE SEEM TO HAVE REACHED A LEAF.

[5]        PAGE←PAGE,FROM
[6]        NEST←NEST,LEVEL
[7]        →EXIT

[8]        ⍝SORT BRANCH BY INCREASING COMPLEXITY...

[9]  MORE:TO←TO[⍋+/TO∘.=XREF[;1]]
[10]       PAGE←PAGE,FROM
[11]       NEST←NEST,LEVEL

[12]       ⍝AND EXPLORE TWIGS.

[13] LOOP:(LEVEL+1) ΔTREE TO[1]
[14]       →(⍴TO←1↓TO)↑LOOP
[15] EXIT:
        ∇
```

Figure 10.6

The rest of workspace documentation falls firmly into the category of 'straightforward but tedious' so I shan't discuss any more of it in detail. Suffice it to say that
you will find the effort involved in writing the necessary functions repaid many
times over.

In this chapter I have referred several times to 'efficient code', because it is in

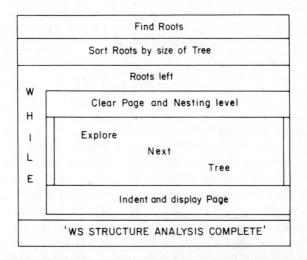

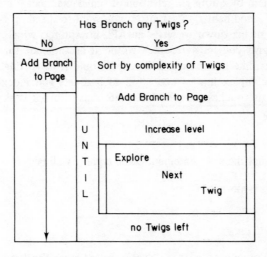

Figure 10.6

system utilities that efficiency matters most. I now want to broaden that view by considering in more detail just how APL works, and how you can make the best use of those precious CPU seconds.

Chapter 11

Efficiency in APL

One of the recurring themes in this book has been that you – the programmer – are a more expensive and valuable resource to your company than is its computer. In this chapter I want to put this consideration temporarily into abeyance, and to look at some ways and means of making your APL code go faster. When trying to code efficient APL you have a twofold problem to face: your code must drive the interpreter; and its code must drive the CPU. Very often the twin objectives (efficient interpretation and efficient execution) are incompatible, and it is rarely clear where the best balance lies between them. In order to shed some light on the problem I am first going to discuss the way APL is interpreted, and what really happens when a function executes. Then I want to give you a feel for the 'interpretation versus execution' problem by quoting a selection of timed examples. Finally I shall round off with a list of 'good habits' to get into if you want to speed up your APL code.

If you were sitting down to write an APL interpreter, which part of it would you expect to give you most trouble? Would it be the code for the obscure and strange functions, like transpose and encode? Would it be sorting out the order of execution in a complex line of code, full of brackets and indexing? In fact it is neither: the single toughest nut the interpreter has to crack is exemplified by the innocent-looking

```
A←3 4ρι12
```

The problem is that the next statement could equally well be

```
A←500 50ρ'RABBITS '
```

and the next

```
A←ι0
```

No conventional computer language gives a programmer this kind of freedom, and APL pays dearly for its flexibility. In a language such as PL/1, you would say

DECLARE A CHARACTER (20);

somewhere towards the start of the program. The compiler would take in turn all such 'DECLARE' statements, and would allocate a suitable chunk of storage for each object you had named. There those objects would remain until the program came to an end, and any references to them would be treated simply as requests to fetch from (or write to) the appropriate area of storage.

APL cannot do this, because it cannot assume that it will always need the same amount of storage for an object just because it happens to have the same name. Consequently it cannot simply replace a name by its location; it must maintain a constantly updated register of names, together with the most recent address of each. As names are used and re-used, the objects to which they refer will migrate around the available workspace, constantly re-occupying old slots as these become vacant. Exactly how interpreters find the available spaces is a subject well beyond the scope of this book, for one thing there are nearly as many different ways of doing it as there are interpreters! How they remember where an object is - and what it looks like - is the subject I want to move to next.

To return to the example a page or so back; you log on to the system, get a clear APL workspace, and type

```
A←3 4ρι12
```

By doing so, you have created an object with a given data type (numeric), rank (2), and shape (3,4); you have established that the symbol 'A' refers to a variable; and you have ensured that any future reference to that symbol will recover from memory the matrix you assigned to it. To deal with all this, APL needs two things:

- The SYMBOL TABLE tells it which names are currently defined, whether they refer to functions or variables, and where the objects in question are currently hiding.

- A DATA DESCRIPTOR is attached to each and every variable, and tells APL all it needs to know about the nature of that variable.

In the case of the example just described, if we subsequently type

```
FRED←20ρ'ABC '
```

then the symbol table and workspace will look rather like

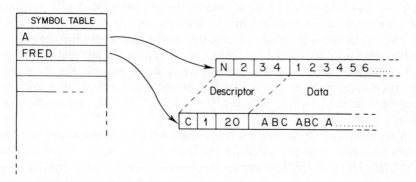

Not all interpreters, incidentally, hold the descriptors with the data in this way. Although they give themselves yet another pointer (from the descriptor to the data itself) to hold, they do gain considerably on operations like ravel and transpose, because these can be done without touching the actual data at all.

To see why this dynamic data management can be so costly, let's look at a simple program line as it would be tackled by APL and by PL/1:

APL	*PL/1*
`I←I+1`	$I = I + 1;$
Look up 'I' in the symbol table. Fetch it from that address; check its data type, shape. Add 1 to it. Find some free memory. Put the result there. Set the symbol table entry for 'I' to that address.	Fetch (address of I) value. Increment it. Store (address of I) result.

The PL/1 version is essentially three assembler instructions; I don't know how many the APL version is, but it is obviously many, many more than that. To appreciate just what a killer this storage management can be, here are two apparently equivalent ways of approaching a common programming task. The object of the exercise is to read up to 1000 records (each of 80 bytes) from a file, and to store them in a character matrix. The two approaches are

Method 1	*Method 2*
`M←0 80ρ' '`	`M←1000 80ρ' '`
`M←M,[1] INPUT`	`M[CT;]←INPUT`
	`M←((CT-1),80)↑M`

The point about Method 1 is that every time a record is read, *all* the previous input is moved to a new area of store. Consequently its CPU consumption is roughly proportional to the square of the number of records read in; Method 2 only moves 'M' once – right at the end – and its CPU use only goes up linearly. I hope Figure 11.1 leaves you suitably terrified – it certainly shocked me when I first drew it!

Having sorted out its storage problems, the next thing the interpreter must do is to disentangle your code into commands which it can execute. For the straightforward arithmetic functions this is simple enough, and the time taken to execute them varies as much as one might expect (Table 11.1) from the intrinsic 'hardness' of each.

When we move into the realms of the more complex 'data management' functions, then a good rule of thumb is that the less general the function, the quicker it will tend to go. This is nicely illustrated by the three data-selection processes following:

- 'Take' is the simplest of the three. It is limited to abstracting a contiguous block of data from one corner of a target array.

- 'Compression' can select rows (or columns) from anywhere in the body of a table, but only in the order in which they originally occurred. It is also limited

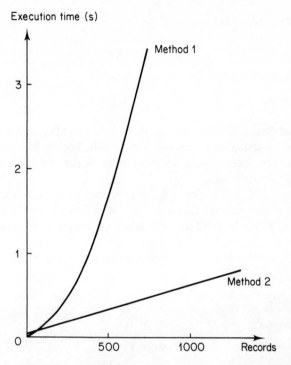

Figure 11.1 Execution time versus number of input records. Timings are given in 3032 CPU seconds

Table 11.1

Function	Time with A fn B	A←?1000ρ10 B←?1000ρ10
+ ⌈ ⌊ =	2 ms	
- |	4 ms	
×	5 ms	
÷ ∈	15 ms	
*	29 ms	
+/A×A	11 ms	
+/A*2	12 ms	

(assuming your system doesn't have 'replicate') to taking each selected row once only.

- 'Indexing' can take as many copies as you want of any row, in any order whatsoever.

It is not too surprising to find that of the three 'take' is about twice as fast as 'compress', which is about twice as fast as 'indexing':

```
M←100 500ρ'RABBITS '
```

M1←M[ι3;]	1.4 ms
M1←((1↑ρM)↑3ρ1)/M	0.69 ms
M1←(3,1↓ρM)↑M	0.29 ms

All three expressions will select the top three rows of a table, but the generality of 'compress' and 'indexing' is not required to do this. For clarity, however, there is no denying that the version using 'indexing' is by far the best of the three, and it is the one I would normally use.

So much for APL in its desk-calculator mode; when you execute a defined function then several further things happen, all of which have some bearing on efficiency. As an example, consider the following sequence of operations:

```
      R←A PLUS B          define a function called 'PLUS'
      ----------
  [1]   R←A+B
       ∇
```

A←'CAT'	store 'A'
P←6	store 'P'
5 PLUS P	execute 'PLUS'
11	result is displayed

When you have defined 'PLUS', 'A', and 'P', the workspace will look like this:

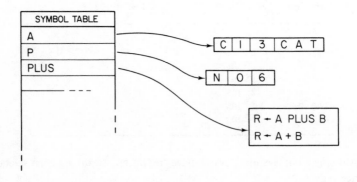

As soon as 'PLUS' is invoked, several things happen:

- Because it uses 'A' to represent one argument, PLUS will need a symbol-table entry for it. To preserve the original value of 'A' (i.e. 'CAT') the old pointer is saved on the STACK.

- At the same time, 'B' is put on the symbol table, with a pointer to the same place as 'P'.

- A work area is then set up, containing the value 5, and pointed to by 'A'.

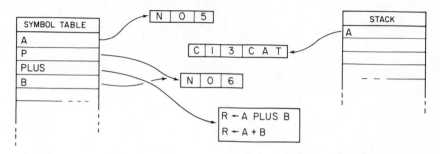

Execution now proceeds, resulting in a further entry 'R' in the symbol table, pointing to an object with a value of 11. Notice that if you had at any stage modified 'B' inside the function, it would have been forced to take an extra copy, otherwise it would also have changed 'P'!

Finally the whole process unwinds:

- The pointer to 'A' is restored from the stack.

- The pointer to 'B' is cleared (but the entry does stay on the symbol table).

- The result is returned (and printed) and the pointer to 'R' is also cleared.

I never knew life was so complicated: imagine what happens at the bottom of a tree of 10 function calls! On second thoughts, don't - one neurotic APL programmer is enough!!

One way of measuring the overhead of function call is to take a recursively defined function, and expand it into a simple repetitive form:

```
      SERIES←SOFAR FIB N                    recursive
      ------------------
[1]    →(N=ρ,SERIES←SOFAR)↑0
[2]    SERIES←(SOFAR,+/¯2↑SOFAR) FIB N
      ∇
```

```
      SERIES←FIB1 N                         repetitive
      -------------
[1]    SERIES←,1
[2]    →(N=ρSERIES)↑0
[3]    SERIES←SERIES,+/¯2↑SERIES
[4]    →(N=ρSERIES)↑0
[5]    SERIES←SERIES,+/¯2↑SERIES
[6]    .........etc.
      ∇
```

Figure 11.2 compares the execution times of the two versions for a variety of values of N. Two points to note are as follows:

138

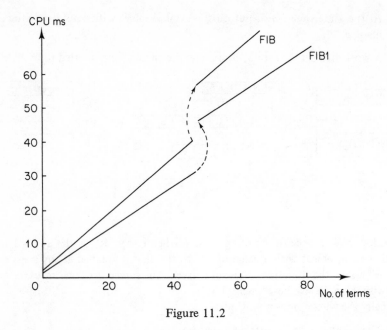

Figure 11.2

- The discontinuity at $N = 47$ is caused by the switch to floating-point arithmetic.

- The overhead is actually quite surprisingly low; not more than 0.2 ms per function call at the most.

Incidentally, an iterative version of FIB1 executes in very much the same times as its repetitive counterpart.

You will remember from Chapter 4 that any program can be structured into one of the following: sequential; alternative; iterative. In APL the beauty of the altern-ative structure is that only the path which is taken needs to be interpreted. On the other hand, the code in an iterative structure will be interpreted every time the algorithm loops around. Moral: branches are fine as long as they are used to select from a range of options, not to iterate over the same piece of code again and again. For example, to display 'TRUE' or 'FALSE' depending on the result of a test, we could use

```
(*\2ρTEST)/'TRUE ',[0.5] 'FALSE'      1.15 ms
```

or

```
       →TEST↓SKIP                      1.08 ms
       'TRUE'
       →END
SKIP:'FALSE'
 END:'READY'
```

I agree that the non-branching form is often clearer, but it may be marginally slower, as in the case above. The same applies to the use of 'execute' to avoid branching: here I personally would almost always opt for the branch as being the more efficient of the two.

Of course even when the interpreter has finished with your code, the resulting assembler still has to be executed, and it is almost impossible to separate the time taken by each phase. What you can do is to compare some alternative ways of achieving the same result, and to try and get some feel for the balance between interpretation and execution. Consider the following two ways of generating prime numbers from 1 to N:

```
      PRIMES←PR N
      -----------
[1]   PRIMES←(2=+/0=(ιN)∘.|ιN)/ιN
      ∇
```

```
      PP←ERATOS N;LAST;D
      ------------------

[1]       ⍝PRIME NUMBERS BY THE SIEVE OF ERATOSTHENES

[2]       PP←1+ιN-1
[3]       LAST←N*÷D←2
[4]   MASK:→(LAST<D)↑0
[5]       PP←((D=PP)∨0≠D|PP)/PP
[6]       D←PP[1+PPιD]
[7]       →MASK

[8]       ⍝ORIGINAL FROM APL\360 PRIMER
[9]       ⍝PAGE 160

      ∇
```

The algorithm using 'the mask of Eratosthenes' progressively masks out large numbers of potential primes at each iteration; consequently it does far fewer comparisons and residues in all. The difference between them is really quite dramatic – see Table 11.2.

Table 11.2

N	PR	ERATOS
10	3	4
50	24	7
100	94	11
200	358	15
500	WS FULL	33
1000	WS FULL	62

In fact, out of curiosity, I coded a version of ERATOS in PL/1 and the result was quite interesting (Figure 11.3). Which line do you think represents the APL, and which the compiled PL/1? In fact the APL is the lower line of the two; it

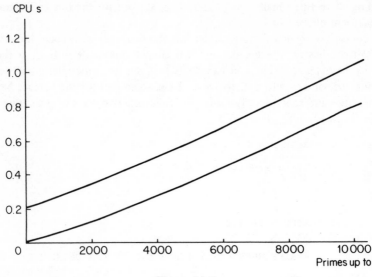

Figure 11.3

consistently uses some 200 ms less than the PL/1 equivalent! I leave you to draw your own conclusions.

This policy of progressively reducing data by successive iterations pays dividends in many other areas. String-searching is one I've already mentioned (ΔSS in Chapter 8), but a more general use might be in the selection of data based on a series of conditions:

```
PERSONNEL WHERE (AGE>35) AND SALARY≤5000
```

Rather than creating complete masks for each condition, 'anding' them, then compressing, it might well be better to take a step-by step approach:

```
WORK←( ..conditional expression.. )/DATA

WORK←( ..conditional expression.. )/WORK
```

etc. This method certainly pays off when you want to remove duplicates from a list which has relatively few unique elements. For example in a 500 × 2 table, with only eight unique rows (see Chapter 8 for a listing of 'UNIQUE'):

```
MAT←(1 1 ⍉<\MAT∧.=⍉MAT)/MAT          2.8 s

MAT←UNIQUE MAT                        31 ms
```

This last example really illustrates the need to think about everything you do in APL; in FORTRAN or PL/1 you are talking about a factor of two or three separating the inefficient from the efficient, in APL it may be a factor of 1000!

I hope these examples will help you to get at least a qualitative impression of the way you can trade off the interpreter's time against overall execution time. However, I don't think that there can ever be any substitute for your own experience; write yourself a function such as

```
TIME FN;ADJ;T
-------------
```

```
[1]   ATIME SPECIFIED OPERATION

[2]    T←⎕AI[2]
[3]    ADJ←⎕AI[2]-T
[4]    T←⎕AI[2]
[5]    ⍎FN
[6]   'TIME WAS ',(⍕T←(⎕AI[2]-T)-ADJ),' MS'
      ∇
```

and get into the habit of investigating functions as you write them. You will certainly give yourself a few surprises, but it won't be long before you develop a pretty accurate instinct for the quickest of a range of possibilities. Incidentally this is one area where APL really scores over a batch system – in APL you can *see* a function which is crawling. It never really bothered me whether my PL/1 jobs took 1 s or 30 s of CPU; if you're waiting 3 h for a batch run you don't tend to fret about the odd 5 min of run-time! In APL a dialogue can stand or fall by response times, and the incentive to drive the machine as fast as possible is very powerful indeed – slow systems irritate users and stand a very good chance of being thrown out! When did you last hear of a batch system being abandoned because it used too much CPU?

Having looked in detail at many of the factors which influence the speed (or otherwise) of an APL program, I now want to offer some rather more general advice on ways of speeding up your APL code.

- *Point 1.* The amount of worry due to any piece of APL code is directly proportional to the number of times it is executed. It sounds obvious, but it is all too easy to spend hours optimizing the code in an obscure error routine which may never be called. When you are trying to speed up code, a valid assumption is that users don't make mistakes!

- *Point 2.* Keep it simple. The more exotic the APL primitive, the less the chance that someone has bothered to optimize it! Stick to the common inner products where you can, and beware of flights of fancy with the outer products and dyadic transpose. Don't be afraid to split complex expressions over two or three lines, and don't be afraid of loops where the alternative involves the creation of large redundant objects.

- *Point 3.* Look out for quirks in the interpreter. Division of zero by zero is a good example:

```
A←(200ρ 2.34 0) ÷ 200ρ 5.67 0        1.25 s
A←(200ρ 2.34 5) ÷ 200ρ 5.67 8        ~ 10 ms
```

- *Point 4.* In general 'closed-form' code is better than looping code. I hope the exceptions in this chapter will serve to prove this particular rule. The same applies to the use of null operations (see Chapter 4) to obviate the use of branching, but again you should be aware of the exceptions.

142

- *Point 5.* Be aware of the way APL shuffles storage around. In particular, it always pays to use indexed assignment into a pre-allocated matrix if you know beforehand how many elements to expect.

- *Point 6.* Don't get carried away trying to make APL look like a bastardized version of PL/1. For example you could define 'IF' and 'THEN' functions to allow expressions like:

```
IF 'LINECT>60' THEN '∆NEWPAGE PC←PC+1 <> LINECT←0'
```

Let a good notation stand on its own two feet, and don't insult it with this sort of miscegenation! The statement above is much better left as

```
   →(LINECT>60)↓QK
   LINECT←0
   ∆NEWPAGE PC←PC+1
QK: ...
```

etc., which will execute a lot faster into the bargain.

- *Point 7.* Keep a reasonable amount (say 50K–100K) of workspace free; some APL functions switch to much slower alternatives if you constrain them too tightly. You may also find that the storage management runs quicker if it has a reasonable freedom of choice.

- *Point 8.* Take advantage of full-screen management. Any application which involves complex data editing will probably be five to 10 times faster if the screen is used properly. Chapter 9 gives more details, and some examples.

- *Point 9.* Don't over-validate. Users are intelligent, careful people who occasionally hit wrong keys. It just isn't worth spending CPU cycles protecting them from strange exotics like

```
2.‾3      or      ‾2‾3
```

which would slip through a simple-minded numeric check. If you have error-trapping then use it as the final long-stop; otherwise be prepared for the (very occasional) phone call when someone manages an 'EXECUTE SYNTAX ERROR'. They won't do it again!

- *Point 10.* Educate your users. This applies particularly to full-screen systems, where it might be possible to do half an hour's work without a single depression of the 'Enter' key. Make sure users know that they don't need to 'Enter' every time they finish a field! In teletype systems you can still pick up some CPU by ensuring that everyone makes the best use of command stacks, abbreviated prompts, etc.

That ends this chapter on efficient use of CPU time. The next chapter covers the related topic of efficient use of storage: often this too can be traded off against CPU time, and I shall again try to show where the balance lies.

Chapter 12

Managing the workspace

In this chapter I am going to discuss two loosely related topics: structuring your data to make the best possible use of the workspace available, and getting at data which lies elsewhere in your computer system. First let me apologise in advance to all those who are exponents of data analysis. In my discussion of APL data structures I shall be forced into some thoroughly unrigorous treatment of a very exact discipline, and I hope you will forgive the trespass on your territory.

Structuring APL Data

It may be that you have the kind of brain that will cope happily with abstractions, and that a discussion based on *n*-tuples, entities, and relations is all you want to see. Personally I find it quite impossible to visualize data in such abstract terms, so I am going to sacrifice rigour for comprehensibility, and confine myself firmly to 'real-world' examples.

The simplest possible representation of data is what we might call the 'card-file' model. Let us represent the sales of six products in four areas, month by month over a series of years:

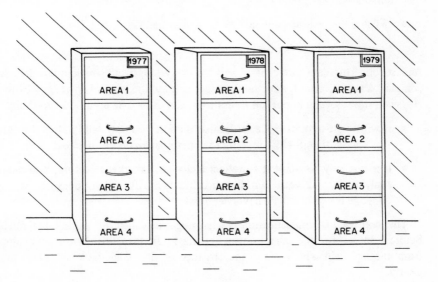

Each cabinet contains the data for a whole year, and has one drawer for each of the four sales areas:

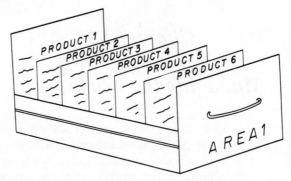

In each drawer there are six divisions (one for each product), and within each division there are 12 cards, recording the sales details (quantity, price, comments, etc.) for the product in that month.

To represent such a structure in APL is simplicity itself:

```
SALES← 0 4 6 12ρ0

SALES←SALES,[1] YEARONE
```

etc., and similarly for PRICE and any other quantities.

It is also absurdly easy to answer questions such as the following:

- 'What did we sell in Area 2 in Year 3?'

```
ANS←+/,SALES[3;2;;]
```

- 'Can I have the figures for March for Product 5?'

```
SUBSET←SALES[;;5;3]
```

- 'What is the highest value sale we have ever made in Area 1?'

```
⌈/,SALES[;1;;]×PRICE[;1;;]
```

And so on. This data model is superb for everything from simple query to quite complex analysis, and I have used it successfully for a number of applications. However, it has several important limitations, and cannot be used for everything:

- It will waste a lot of space for 'sparse' data. If you only sell Product 3 in Area 2 in Spring, then SALES is going to contain an awful lot of zeros!

- It is not easy to adapt it to reflect a change in market structure. You cannot easily replace all your four-drawer cabinets by five-drawer ones just because someone has pioneered a new sales area!

The next level of sophistication is what might be called the 'single-table' model. Before I show how the sales information might fit into this, here is an example from another field which shows the elegance of the 'single-table' approach more clearly.

To keep a record of a company's employee details, the data structure could be

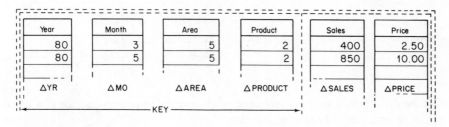

Emp. no.	Name	Salary	Age	Department
A 4321	JONES A	5000	35	ACCOUNTS
C 2406	SMITH C	7500	46	COMPUTER
ΔEMP	ΔNAME	ΔSALARY	ΔAGE	ΔDEPT

◄— KEY —►

Here each 'data entity' is held in a single APL variable, which may be a simple vector (ΔSALARY) or a character matrix (even better a vector of vectors; see 'Nested arrays' in Chapter 14). The complete details of each employee can be found by selecting the corresponding elements (or rows) from each object in turn. Each row can be identified uniquely by a 'Key' variable or variables (ΔEMP in this case).

As a structure for data enquiry, the single-table model is again simple and effective:

- 'What is the average salary of employees over 35?'

```
AVERAGE (ΔAGE>35)/ΔSALARY
```

- 'How many people work in Accounts?'

```
+/ΔDEPT∧.='ACCOUNTS'
```

- 'Can I have a list of all employees, in order of salary?'

```
LIST←(ΔEMP,' ',ΔNAME)[⍋ΔSALARY;]
```

Applied to the 'sales-by-area' data, the single-table model gives a considerable economy in storage, at only slight cost in complexity. The model would now look like

Year	Month	Area	Product	Sales	Price
80	3	5	2	400	2.50
80	5	5	2	850	10.00
ΔYR	ΔMO	ΔAREA	ΔPRODUCT	ΔSALES	ΔPRICE

◄————————— KEY —————————►

The main gain is clearly the saving in storage (assuming we only create a table entry for a non-zero sales figure), but this model can also react more easily to new areas and new products. However, simple enquiries and summaries are not quite as simple as they were:

- 'Total of sales, split by area . . .'

```
TOTAL←SALES+.×AREA∘.=⍳⌈/AREA
```

- 'What did product 3 do in June?'

```
SUBSET←((PRODUCT=3)∧MO=6)/YR,[1.5]SALES
```

It also fails to record prices for products that don't sell! The solution to this anomaly (and others like it) is discussed in the next section.

For an application of this type, I would suggest the 'card-file' model where you are interested mainly in enquiry on stable data. The 'single-table' model may be forced on you by lack of workspace, but it does have the advantage of easy updating and modification. A further point in its favour is that it fits in very nicely with the concept of component files; each APL variable becomes one entry on the file and need only be brought into the workspace when required.

I want to concentrate now on the employee-record example, and to develop the single-table model rather further. The first concept to introduce is the 'reference-table', the need for which becomes apparent when you consider questions like

- 'Employees over 30, sorted by department'

- 'Who is responsible to Bloggs?'

The trouble with the single-table model is that it leads to unnecessary repetitions; many employees will work in the same department, and each department will be uniquely associated with a manager. What we must do is remove 'Department' (and anything related to it) to a separate table, linked to the original table by a pointer vector:

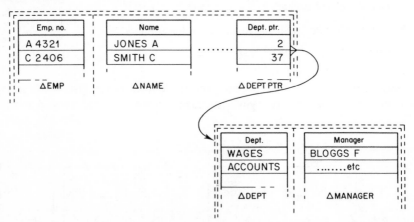

As we shall shortly see, the 'reference table' is really only a special case of a much more general way of linking related data.

The sort by department is now very easy indeed:

```
NAME[⍋ΔDEPTPTR;]
```

but more important is the saving on workspace, and the greater ease with which the main table can be updated. It is obviously vital that every employee has a valid department, and with a reference table this can easily be verified using a function such as ΔLKP (see Chapter 8) which won't even insist on the full department name.

The single-table model would be very vulnerable to

D3351   ACCOUNTS
D3352   ACCOUNTING

where two people have slightly different ideas on the name of the same department. This new model has the additional advantage that it will cope quite happily with the unlikely occurrence of a department which has no employees!

The reference table also allows you to change any department-related information – such as a change of manager – without touching the main table at all, which can be very useful if you are moving data to and from file. So what's the catch?! Well, consider what happens if you want to add a new department between 'Wages' and 'Computer': all the pointers to 'Computer' (and departments following) will have to be increased by one. Similarly, before you delete an entry from a reference table you must first check that nothing is pointing to it; if you delete it anyway, you *must* take some action about any such rows.

Once again we have gained in efficiency of storage and enquiry, but this time the cost is increased complexity during update.

The second refinement to the single-table model is something I would call a 'link table'. Again taking the staff record as my example – suppose we want to keep a training log for each employee. The company has several different courses, on which employees are sent, so one clear requirement is a table for each of these:

Course code	Course description	Duration
A 310	MARKETING	3
A 315	FINANCE	5

The question is, how do we link the employee table to this? Each employee may have been on many (or no) courses; likewise each course will have been attended by varying numbers of employees! A simple pointer system just will not cope, so this is where the link table comes in – it will look like

Staff ptr	Course ptr	Date attended
1	2	01 / 01 / 80
2	2	05/02/76
2	1	03/06/78

i.e. one entry for each occasion any staff member goes on any course, with pointers in *both* directions. Some people/courses will have no entries at all on the link table, some will have many, but each employee-course pair will uniquely identify a date – the date Joe Bloggs was sent to learn about Creative Thinking. The data model now looks like

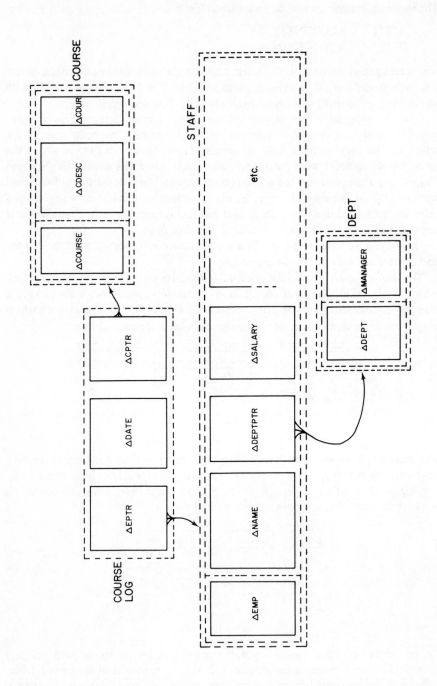

It now becomes clear that the table–table relationship is really only a special case of the more general table–link table: the STAFF–DEPT link could have been defined as

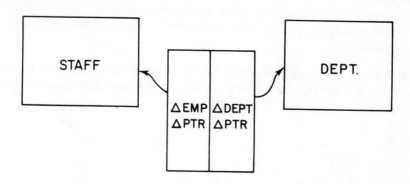

but, because of our insistence that each employee has exactly one department, ΔEMPΔPTR is simply a permutation of $\iota 1 \uparrow \rho \Delta EMP$! Without loss of generality we can sort by employee and put ΔDEPTΔPTR on the end of the employee table.

In my experience, these two elements (table, link table) are ideal building bricks for the typical APL database. I know this approach to data modelling lacks the rigour of a genuine relational analysis, but it almost invariably results in an equivalent representation, it is very easy to handle, and extremely flexible. Because the links follow strict rules (which are independent of the model as a whole), you can use standard code to maintain each type of link.

To maintain the integrity of the data requires the application of only two simple rules:

- When the keys in a table are re-ordered, all pointers (whether from link table or main table) must be changed to match.

- When a row is deleted from a table, then one of two things must happen: anything which previously pointed to it must either be deleted, or must be re-routed to a 'catch-all' row with a value indicating 'unknown'. In general we would probably tolerate such an implicit deletion from a link table (COURSELOG), but not from a main table (STAFF).

Fortunately, both these rules can be obeyed rather easily – the trick goes something like this:

- First create a dummy key (which the user never sees) which is simply the integers from one up to the number of rows in the table.

- Allow the user to make any changes he likes (deleting/adding/re-ordering) to the table; whatever he does to it, you do the same to your dummy key.

- When the changes are complete, you first delete (or re-route) any rows where the corresponding pointer no longer occurs in the dummy key. You then look up the pointer in the dummy key to obtain the new values for that pointer.

At this point it should (I hope!) be becoming clear where the power of this data model lies. It is the interconnections that can bog down any data base system, and this model has only one type of connector:

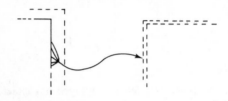

i.e. a many-to-one connector. This means that as long as you stick to these building bricks you can put together a database of considerable complexity, and be confident that it will work! Even more important, you can modify it just as easily – clearly it is a very simple job to add new entities to existing relationships (i.e. new variables to existing tables, pointers or variables to existing link tables, etc.), but it is also not difficult to add completely new tables, or to change the links between existing ones. In fact I have a suspicion that the whole process should be automated: all we need is a conversational database editor to help establish (or change) the relationships, which will then write the code for us. Any volunteers – I've got a book to finish!

This chapter is really about data maintenance, but I clearly cannot escape without some reference to the way that data might be used. First, access is possible through the main table, to produce a list of the courses attended by selected employees:

Employee	Name	Dept	Course	Date attended
A6215	A SMITH	OP RES	CREATIVE THINKING	21/03/79
			FINANCE	03/07/80

The other obvious route to the data is through 'COURSE', to produce a similar list, but showing the employees who attended selected courses:

Course	Description	Attended by	Date
A301	FINANCE	A SMITH	03/07/80
		B JONES	03/07/80

To achieve these results, we need one further component in the data model, but fortunately it obeys the same rules as the bricks we already have - it is the 'selection', which may point to any table, using a simple one-to-one relationship. It could be updated explicitly by functions such as 'SELECT' or 'SORT' and implicitly whenever the table it pointed to were changed.

Obviously there is scope for far more sophisticated selection and presentation of data than I have shown here, but the principle remains the same. By formalizing data in this way, you lay firm foundations for the future evolution of the kind of decision-support system I outlined in Chapter 2. Working within a flexible framework which guarantees the integrity of your base data will give you far greater freedom in that vital phase of 'programming by negotiation'.

In summary, any collection of APL objects can be gathered into logical relationships of only three types:

- *Selections* - which simply pick out rows from tables.

- *Tables* - which consist of a key (usually, but not always, a single variable), and anything related to it. These objects may be simple data, or pointers to other tables. (Pointers are only allowed in the special case where a table entry has one - and only one - corresponding entry on another table.)

- *Link tables* - which consist simply of related objects, where many (or no) rows of a link table may be related to one or more tables. A link table may only be updated through the main-table entries to which it points, and it may be used in displays from any of them.

Having outlined what is effectively a poor man's approach to relational database, I now want to take an equally unrigorous view of relational analysis! Given a bucketful of assorted data, how do you set about sorting it into sensible groups (tables and link tables)?

The first stage is to isolate the key objects which will serve to identify each row. Having done this, you can hook on to these keys anything which is related to them. Anything left will have to find its way into a link table, which is where it gets tricky! I think another example is appropriate here, so here is a bucketful of half-rationalized data:

```
JOB NUMBERS/DESCRIPTIONS
SUPPLIER NUMBER/LOCATION
SUPPLIERS' PRICE LISTS
OUTSTANDING ORDERS TO EACH SUPPLIER
PARTS NEEDED FOR EACH JOB
PART NUMBER/DESCRIPTION/STOCK IN HAND
```

Here I have isolated three tables; this is as far as we can go without some thought as to how the data is going to be used.

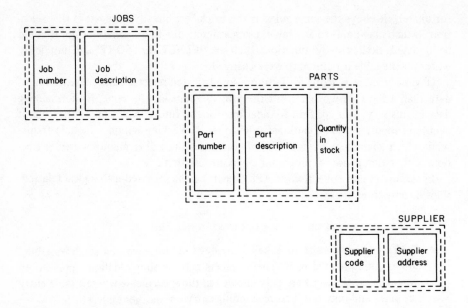

The first obvious view of the data will be that of the engineer, who will see JOBS composed of PARTS obtained from SUPPLIERS:

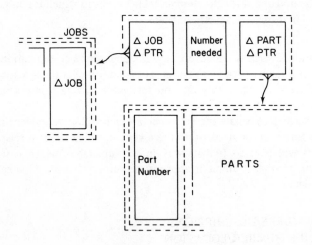

Now many suppliers probably supply the same parts, but at different prices, so the bridge between PARTS and SUPPLIERS must look like

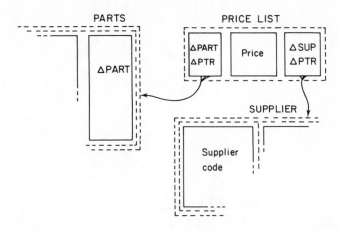

i.e. the price is implied by the combination of part number and supplier; neither will do on its own. This also reflects the view of the buyer, who sees SUPPLIERS with catalogues of PARTS.

Similarly, there may be several ORDERS outstanding (for the same PART) to different SUPPLIERS (The project planning department may well see the data in this light):

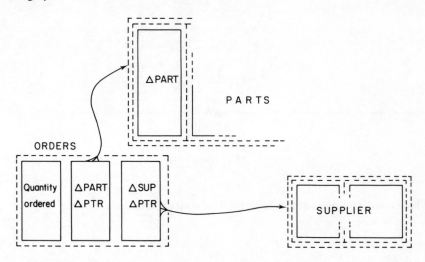

Each ORDER will be the result of a requisition from a particular JOB (the accountant's view?):

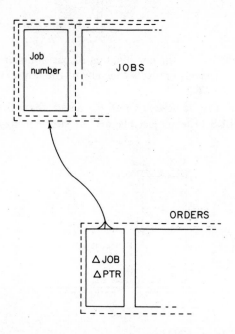

Which completes one possible analysis. This final data model is

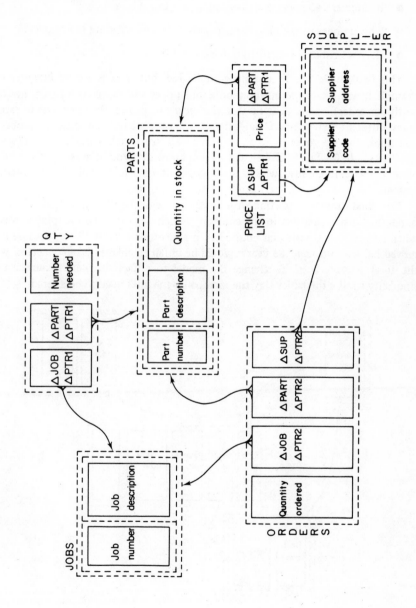

156

But it is by no means the only one for this data. However, it can answer a wide range of queries, such as

- 'If supplier 345 goes on strike, which jobs might be affected?'
- 'Who supplies us with left-handed sprockets, and what are their prices?'
- 'Have we enough widgets to finish Job 678?'

This final model really is quite complicated, but it does ensure integrity (for example it will retain the information about prices and suppliers for parts not currently on order), and it does provide the means to project the same data to satisfy many different viewpoints. Data design is bound to be influenced by the processes you think you are going to do on it; with a well structured relational model (which the PARTS–JOBS–SUPPLIER model is) you know that you have retained the maximum possible flexibility, which is an excellent base from which to negotiate a system.

Two final examples, starting with another view of the EMP-link-COURSE data. Supposing that it matters to the company which department an employee was in when he went on a particular course? In practice this is quite likely, because if he moved halfway through the year it would be unfair to charge his new manager with the total training cost! To change the model to reflect this new requirement is simplicity itself – the tables stay the same; only the links need to be altered:

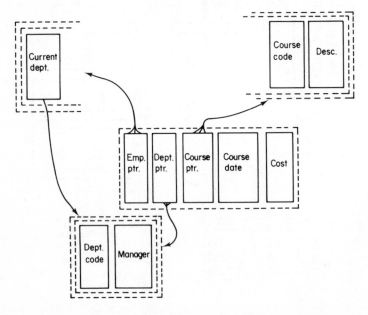

Lastly, there is the old chestnut of plex-structures (parts explosions, critical path networks, etc.). These provide a fascinating example of tables where many entries are related to many entries in the *same* table! Take, for example, workspace documentation:

Chapter 10 (see Figure 10.6) illustrates how easy it is to draw the workspace structure from data stored in this way (having first screened out recursive calls!). Relational analysis may be no more than applied common-sense, but it is a tool no self-respecting APL programmer should be without.

Getting at External Data

I am going to close this chapter with a few notes on a very tricky subject: your company has lots of nice data which you would love to get at from APL – how do you do it? Here are four possible methods, all suitable for slightly different needs:

- Print it out, and key it in again! This is by no means as daft as it sounds; if you are implementing a production planning system for a couple of products, then why bother automating a process that will only take 10 minutes anyway? It also has the advantage that the person doing the keying will have his attention brought to any odd figures as early as possible. The disadvantage is that he might make some typing errors, or might 'bend' some of the figures to what he thinks they 'ought' to be.

- Do a 'one-off' sequential-read, thereafter maintaining the data as above. APL just isn't suited to ploughing through files one record at a time, but you may get away with it once a year. This is a suitable approach when you want to do a detailed analysis on some historical data, which may only change every couple of months anyway.

- Use a conventional APL system to create a batch job (in COBOL, PL/1 or some special purpose database query language) which will go off and do a selective retrieval for you. This subset file will still be in the 'wrong' format, but it will be a far more manageable size than its parent. You can also ask for the output to be blocked up to a reasonable length (e.g. 50 X 80 byte records) to speed APL's access to it. This technique might be used if you wanted to analyse parts of a very large data bank, for example the monthly sales of 200 products over 10 years (say 25 000 records on a conventional file). To find out about left-handed sprockets in 1975 you create a batch job which selects the relevant 12 records (in no time flat if its's PL/1) and places them end to end as a single output record. The overall *elapsed* time for all this is probably less than APL would take simply to read the original file, and the economies in CPU time are enormous.

- Design a general purpose file-inversion program which will accept any sequential file as input, and will use parameters to extract the fields of interest. An excellent repository for the output is IBM's VSAM file system, because you can use your APL variable names as the file keys. For example the inversion of a personnel records file might be represented by

Target File

Name		Age	Sex	
1	20	21 23	24	
SMITH ACD		25	M	
JONES J		17	F	
ROBINSON D		25	M	

Selection Cards

Variable name		Type	Column	Length	
1	12	13	14 15	16 17	
NAME		C	1	20	
AGE		N	21	3	
SEX		C	24	1	

Output File

Key	Last rec.	Type	Field size	Data
1	14	15 16	17 18	19 4096
NAME	01	C	20	SMITH ACD JONES J....
NAME	02 *	C	20	LOGGS F ROBINS K
AGE	01 *	N		25 17 25 56 ......
SEX	01 *	C	1	MFMMF........

Once the output file has been produced, it can be accessed very efficiently from APL, and data can be retrieved conveniently by name:

```
FETCH'AGE,SALARY'
```

```
AVERAGE SALARY WHERE AGE >35
```

where 'FETCH' uses the names supplied to key to the file. My one reservation about file inversion is that it is very difficult to design a program which will deal efficiently with both short, fat files and long, thin files, not to mention a wide variety of database systems. Heavily used data may often justify a specific inverter, tuned for maximum efficiency for that file only.

So I must draw to a close this chapter on data management with APL. It is a fascinating subject, and one which is still very much in its infancy. As workspace sizes increase to hitherto unheard of values (who would have believed 16 megabytes in APL\360's early days?) it is a subject which will become increasingly important, and in five or ten years' time it should be possible to implement quite large databases entirely within the workspace. Now there's a management information tool worth talking about!

Chapter 13

Towards the mechanized office

'Office automation' has been one of the buzzwords of the late 1970s. It conjures up visions of managers deeply involved in an international tele-conference, while their respective secretaries exchange memos on a network of communicating word-processors. All these scenarios abound with technological marvels, each designed to speed up some specific office task, but will they really lead to a more efficient business? I rather doubt it, and the rest of this chapter explains my reservations about this kind of office automation, and outlines the role that I think APL can play in the future mechanization of office functions.

The first thing to realize is that an office does not exist to give people the opportunity to fill in forms, type memos, file documents, etc. It exists to perform some kind of business function (selling things, controlling stocks, invoicing customers), and it does so by making the best use of the available tools (filing cabinets, forms, typewriters, spikes on the wall). Let me quote again part of the passage I quoted in Chapter 2:

> '. . . the sum of the optimal solutions to each component problem is *not* an optimal solution to the mess as a whole.'

All the word-processor optimizes is the process of putting words on paper; it may contribute to an overall improvement in efficiency, but there is no reason why it *should*. In fact it may reduce efficiency by flooding some other office with redundant paperwork! The question we should be asking is not 'What is an office?' but 'Why is an office?' We can then begin to make some progress towards using our techno-logical marvels to improve the overall office *function*, rather than simply speeding up the *tasks* currently used to achieve that function. Unfortunately, this is very easy to say and very difficult to do!

The problem is that there are as many different office functions as there are offices, so we are faced with the daunting prospect of writing specific, high-level tools for each and every office. By focussing on tasks, the manufacturers of word-processors, copying machines, etc., have found a large and lucrative market (tasks being pretty standard things), but I doubt very much if they have contributed the hoped-for gains in overall efficiency. They may indeed have increased 'the number of pages per secretary per day' by some impressive factor, but how much of this 'productivity gain' is really due to Parkinson's law ('Work expands to fill the time available')? They may have doubled the 'pieces of mail logged per hour', but how much of it is piling up elsewhere, unwanted and unread? Such artificial measures of task performance are at best useless, and at worst misleading. To justify any form of office automation we must look for ways of improving the office function, and ways of measuring this in terms of overall business objectives. If you can present a case in the form,

> 'By improving certain production planning functions we can help the company to reduce stocks of materials, whilst also cutting down the number of occasions we run out of finished goods.'

then you should go ahead, even if the actual financial gain is hard to quantify. If your solution can be assembled entirely from generic tools (word-processors, text retrieval systems) available cheaply off the shelf, then so much the better. This might apply to a system at the very top of an organization, say to help the managing director's secretary, but lower down in the murky waters of short-term planning and production management you are most unlikely to find an 'off-the-peg' system. It is here that I come full circle to the philosophy of Chapter 2, and the methodology of Chapter 6; I believe in APL as the ideal, all-purpose, generic tool with which we can build the functionally specific systems needed for true office mechanization, and that really is what this book has been all about.

Before I go on to explain this belief, I must define some of the terms I have so far been using rather too loosely. In particular I must make clear the distinction between (a) a task and a function; (b) automation and mechanization; (c) generic and specific tools. Here I am going to follow the definitions of Hammer and Zisman (1980) from their paper 'Design and implementation of office information systems'.

- A task is a simple, narrowly focussed activity; a function is an end realized by means of task performance. In general, we can say that a *tool* is used to help perform a *task*, and a *system* to help realize a *function*.

- Automation implies the use of machines to replace people; mechanization implies the provision of improved tools to help people to perform tasks better. Examples of true office automation include most of the early DP systems, like payroll and accounting; examples of mechanization would be computer-aided design, visual interactive simulation, etc.

- A generic tool (typewriter, filing cabinet) is not tailored in any way to a particular application; a specific (or custom-built) tool has some knowledge of a particular system built into it – this makes it much more powerful for that particular application, but sacrifices all the economies of scale as a result.

Functional systems are built from some combination of automated and mechanized tasks, using generic tools where available, and specific tools otherwise. With APL we can provide the generic tools (desk calculator, word-processor, data management, text retrieval), and build the specific ones (production scheduling, materials planning, sales forecasting) all within one environment. That is one reason why I believe APL has a future in office automation; another is communication – by this I don't just mean communication between people (although that, after all, is what APL was designed for), but communication between systems.

There seems to me to be one crucial factor missing from many otherwise credible scenarios of our automated future. In the enormous diversity of species emerging from the primal slime of the electronics revolution, there is an almost wilful desire to invent new protocols, new data formats; we are building a Tower of Babel to dwarf its biblical predecessor into total insignificance! The mathematics of the situation is straightforward enough: in a network of N nodes, the number of edges is given by

```
EDGES←.5×N×N-1
```

It is the implications of this innocent-looking formula that we must not overlook. Consider a company, already the proud possessor of a word-processor, which purchases a similar machine from a different manufacturer and wants to link the two. It now has two nodes, one edge, and requires one protocol-converter. Should it purchase a third machine, it will have three nodes, and three edges; a company with 10 such devices has 10 nodes and up to 45 edges to its network. To add just one more box could trigger a demand for 10 more interfaces; already a large proportion of the total processing power of the network is being consumed internally, and as more nodes are added its productivity will tend rapidly to zero. Of course no company would deliberately get itself into such a mess; the trouble is that each machine is bought separately to satisfy a *local* need; it is not until later that someone sees the possibility of linking them up, and by then it is too late to change.

Perhaps we could learn a lesson from the early days of the British Empire in Africa: when a 50 mile stretch of railway was laid in Egypt, it was built to the same gauge as a similar length near Durban, some 4000 miles away! I don't know if they ever did link up, but at least the potential was there. APL many not be the ideal solution to your word-processing problems, it may not be the best text-retrieval tool on the market, but it can at least do *all* these things reasonably well. What's more it can share data effortlessly across an unlimited number of apparently unrelated applications, allowing wholly unexpected fusions and cross-fertilization to occur. No longer will it be necessary to copy figures laboriously from computer printouts, simply to have them re-keyed as part of a 'neat' report. The text of Chapter 8 exemplifies just this point: using my '∆' editor as a word-processor I have gone from executable (and tested) APL code straight to the printed page, with no manual intervention in between. The advantages are a considerable saving in time and effort, but more importantly a guaranteed freedom from transcription errors. Providing such a service for a production planning department may give a far better return in timeliness and accuracy than the most sophisticated of OR models!

Here, then, is my scenario for the future; it is (of course) an idealization, and I shall list the snags in a moment, but it does at least give us something at which to aim. First, I would like to see a far greater dispersion of the hardware; a series of APL processors, each capable of supporting something akin to APL∗PLUS, with say 16 megabytes of active workspace. Each processor would support *one* user (the only way I know of getting consistent response times), and data local to an application would reside with that processor, being sent down the line for backup as required. Apart from this, communication would be limited to 'electronic mail', large printouts destined for a central pool of fast printers, and central data shared by a number of users. Tasks such as workspace documentation would also run in the centre, being triggered from the appropriate user by means of shared variables, and thereafter run 'off-line' from his point of view.

New applications will be designed by a team of programmer-analysts, who will follow the approach of Chapter 6 to develop systems which address the functional needs of the organization. They will also be responsible for detecting the need for new generic tools (or 'packages' if you prefer) and for enhancing and maintaining those already on the shelf. This team will also play a co-ordinating role in organizing regular APL workshops, and generally keeping in touch with the APL community. As an increasing number of users begin to do their own programming, the workshop will supply the need for an efficient clearing house for APL gossip; it will be a place for new users to get advice and for old hands to test each others' APL wits.

So much for the ideal; what of the reality? Well the hardware I don't really see as a problem; I've given up being astonished at processor powers that double every three years. In fact the more we can structure the system to minimize user-to-user communication the easier it will be to maintain. There is always the danger that, for example, a production planner will come to take for granted the availability of a nearby printer belonging to the payroll system. Because he has never made a *formal* arrangement to use it, he has no real grievance if it is taken away, but I doubt if that will stop him becoming more than a little upset!

Informally shared hardware is one problem, shared data (whether formally or informally) is another. By this I don't mean the problems of controlling shared access to files - these have already been well and truly solved - rather the conflicts that can arise between members of a user community who each have a different perspective on the same data. Consider the 'employees–courses' database discussed in Chapter 12. From the point of view of the training department, the data looks like

Course	*People requiring it*
SKIN DIVING	JONES, SMITH
CREATIVE THINKING	BLOGGS, HARRIS, SMITH

The training department's objectives will include (a) scheduling courses round the known workload of the tutors and (b) ensuring a reasonable number of participants at each course. On the other hand, each manager will see the schedule as a way of completing his staff's education at the least cost in departmental productivity. He will be concerned to avoid the possibility that both co-authors of a critical system may be away simultaneously, and so on. In fact to him the data looks like

Employee	*Time committed to . . .*
SMITH	Creative Thinking, Skindiving
HARRIS	Creative Thinking

We cannot allow indiscriminate access and updating by both parties; even in a system as simple as this there are clearly visible the seeds of anarchy. In more complex databases there may be dozens of different projections of the data, and some formal way of detecting and resolving conflicts must be invented.

These ideas were first (to my knowledge anyway) developed by a colleague in OR – Richard Thomas. As his work is as yet unpublished, I have asked his permission to quote from it here. He calls the concept 'Distributed Decision Making', and with it sets out to meet these ideals:

> 'Everybody does their own thing, and yet organizational goals are still reached. The point is that you make a decision based on your perception of reality, and diffferent people will view the same reality differently. We must try to design an information system so that it lets people see a view of reality within which they can take decisions; these decisions then get incorporated into the information system, and some people may notice them depending on their own reality.'

How is this to be achieved? Well, Richard sees the following constructs as fundamental:

- *Database*: all the data.

- *Window:* a designed view of the data.

- *Decision realm:* what we allow people to update through a window.

- *Doing box:* a personal computing system, linked to the database through a window, which helps a person to do his job.

- *Conflict resolver:* facilities to detect and resolve opposing decisions, for example to act as arbiter when a variable is oscillating as a result of two or more people using their 'doing boxes' in opposing ways. This could simply take the form of exception reports to the appropriate managers.

His design method closely parallels mine, with the one important addition that where multiple users are involved some criteria for the existence of conflict will need to be established. Once this has been done (and the database, its windows and decision realms in place, has been set up), then the 'doing boxes' can evolve in close conjunction with the system's users.

At present, I have absolutely no idea how I should set about implementing such a system! All I can offer is the haziest of notions that if there is one single tool which just *might* prove up to the task, it is the APL shared variable. Let us imagine an APL workspace controlling the database. The decision realms correspond to functions within that workspace, and each window to a pair of functions communicating by shared variables:

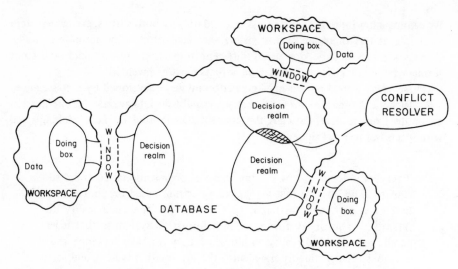

One member of the pair is in the host computer, the other is embedded in the user's own workspace, forming part of his 'doing box'. Of course this may also use his personal, local data, and it may have other windows to other databases. I know this already slips away from Richard's definition of the database as 'all the data', but I feel obliged to compromise this one principle to bring the whole idea within manageable bounds. The 'conflict resolver' is really a special kind of 'doing box' which may even be empowered to alter other people's decision realms when it detects certain pre-set conditions.

Will it ever be done? Not with today's hardware I'm sure, but given another 10 years and a few good brains to worry at it and I think we might see something of the kind emerging. I shall follow its progress with interest!

I shall now try to summarize in one paragraph the most important points in this chapter. First, true office mechanization demands a view of office function in the context of the whole organization. To achieve real productivity gains we shall probably be forced to forsake generality, and to create specific tools suitable for a very limited range of applications. Secondly, I believe in APL as an excellent way of providing such tools, whilst also making available more general facilities such as text editing and data retrieval. Thirdly, I don't think we yet possess either the technology or the expertise to implement such 'holistic' systems effectively. I propose the ideas of 'distributed decision making', implemented using stand-alone APL processors and shared variables, as a possible pathway towards the future.

Chapter 14

Whither APL

The short answer is 'I don't know', but I'm as willing to take a few guesses as the next man! APL stands where it does today as much in spite of as because of the efforts of IBM, and even that paragon of capitalist efficiency seems unsure what to do next. Having attempted briefly to sell APL on the 'personal computing for managers' ticket, they now seem to be basing their marketing effort largely round APL packages. The time-sharing bureaux, on the other hand, have gone hell-for-leather to corner the market in sophisticated data manipulation and econometric modelling. By making available vast databases of valuable information (and a file-management system to access them) they have clearly established a permanent, and very profitable, business.

Where does that leave the rash of one-off commercial systems I have described in this book? Not on time-sharing bureaux, certainly, because of the problems of telephone lines, and the need to get at company data. On some IBM system on your own computer? Well yes, but wouldn't it be nice to have all those goodies like component files and □FMT! On an APL mini, or micro? These are clearly the jokers in the pack but haven't yet appeared in sufficient numbers to make a real impact. The microprocessor of the moment is the Z-80, an eight-bit machine, which just doesn't have the muscle to implement a full-scale APL system. Try writing the assembler for floating-point division and you'll quickly see why! On the other hand there is at least one excellent mini-computer APL system already on the market, and the next generation of micros is on the horizon. These will be 16-bit devices, and will include hardware functions to do the complex arithmetic. They should also have features which make screen-handling a positive pleasure; even in Z-80 assembler it is quite absurdly easy to put together a fascinating variety of 'video games'. Someone, however, will have to hurry: BASIC is already far too well established to be easily dislodged, and unless there is a good micro-APL soon it will be too late to make any difference.

If APL does miss out on the micro-computer scene it will be a big loss both for APL and for the micros. Its sheer compactness makes it an excellent candidate for programs which have to be shoe-horned into 2K or 3K of memory, and its matrix-handling will make light of video-tennis or 'Space Invaders' or whatever. Also the shared variable concept seems ideal for a wide variety of process-control applications – why shouldn't you share a variable with your central heating system?! This process-control tack is one I shall return to shortly, but first a brief review of what is happening back in the APL mainstream.

There would seem to be three parallel streams of development: in the language itself; in the environment within which it is run; and in the applications people are using it for. Sometimes the first two of these overlap, for example VS APL regards file access as a feature of the environment, whereas in APL*PLUS it comes as part of the language. For consistency I shall follow IBM on this one, and classify anything not available in VS APL as part of the environment.

First then, the APL notation itself. There has been astonishingly little change in this since APL\360 gained format, execute, and scan, and became APLSV. In the early days APL *was* IBM, and any change to the language was, by definition, adopted universally. Today it is more difficult, and anyone who invents a really worthwhile extension to the notation is going to have a hard job persuading all the manufacturers to adopt it. Two recent examples spring to mind: APL*PLUS with 'Replicate' as an obvious (when someone else has thought of it!) extension of 'Compress':

```
      1 2 0 1/'ABCD'

   ABBD
```

The sooner this one goes on general release the better – I have lost count of the number of times I have had to program round it with some wasteful construction. Another interesting idea comes from GEC, with their 4000 series mini-computer APL:

```
      ρB←1 0 1 ωA←3 4ρι12

   3 1 4
```

They have used omega to give a way of expanding the *rank* of an object. This makes the vector to one-column matrix job a great deal easier:

```
   MAT←1 0 ωVEC
```

and, combined with their more relaxed view of conformability, we can multiply a matrix by a vector very simply:

```
   MAT←MAT×1 0ωVEC           by column

   MAT←MAT×0 1ωVEC           by row
```

The problem with this is that alpha and omega are already spoken for by Ken Iverson for his idea of direct functional definition, so here is one for the international committees to chew over. Incidentally, why has no one ever copied the Burroughs 700 construction:

```
   MAT←MAT+[1] VEC

   MAT←MAT×[2] VEC
```

with the default of [2], i.e. the last dimension? It can't be that difficult to let all the scalar dyadics take an axis operator.

Two other things to mention are the use of 'diamond' to put several statements on each line, and the ability (available on APL\360 and lost thereafter) to append comments to existing lines of code. Both of these make obvious sense when you are working with a screen 79 columns wide but only 24 rows deep. Few APL statements go beyond column 30, and it is an absurd waste to have to add extra lines for comments when there is ample space in the right-hand margin. In fact I have almost given up commenting the body of the code, confining myself to a hefty comment at the top of the function. I find it more helpful to be able to see the entire function on one screen than to have each line individually described. For one thing, it is not always obvious if a comment refers to the line immediately above, or immediately below!

The same applies to the use of 'diamond', with the additional advantage that this can be used to group logically related statements. For example, if 'STOCK' and 'SALES' have been passed to a function as rows of 'INFO',

```
      PROD←SCHED INFO;STK;SLS
      - - - - - - - - - - - - - - - - - - - - - -

[1]    ⍝SCHEDULE PRODUCTION TO MEET EXPECTED DEMAND

[2]    STK←INFO[1;] <> SLS←INFO[2;]

             .
             .
             .
```

etc., not only saves space, but adds considerably to readability.

Finally 'nested arrays', which may be the most exciting language development of all. The one area where I have always found APL rather weak (at least in comparison with PL/1) is when handling structures of data. For example the staff table of Chapter 12 contains a variety of disparate APL objects:

ΔEMP	numeric vector
ΔNAME	character matrix
ΔSALARY	numeric vector

The process of compressing across 'STAFF' is made tedious by the necessity to treat each object individually; if it were possible to create a *matrix* consisting of vectors 'ΔEMP, ΔNAME', each enclosing the contents of the 'nested' variable,

```
      STAFF←MASK/STAFF
```

would be a far more natural (as well as more concise) way of removing a row. Similarly, to select employees earning over £5000:

```
      (5000<⊃STAFF[3;])/STAFF[;1 2]
```

For more details, see Smith "Nested arrays: the tool for the future", one of a number of papers collected in a volume entitled *APL in Practice* (Wiley, 1980).

The next thing to look at is the APL environment, and here I am going to include all the borderline cases like system functions and system variables. As far as the hardware itself goes, the slogan seems to be 'bigger, faster, cheaper'; APL will benefit from all of these, but particularly from 'bigger'; as core is replaced by fast

170

semiconductor memory, APL's voracious appetite for workspace will finally be sated. There are two other hardware developments I shall follow with particular interest: ICL's distributed array processor and (also at ICL) content-addressable memory. DAP could suddenly transform APL from being on a par with conventional language to being about two orders of magnitude faster; CAM is the ideal vehicle for the APL relational database from Chapter 12. In fact '∧.=' effectively is CAM, but in core!

Looking now at operating systems, I find myself relentlessly drawn back to IBM. It is their declared intention to make VS APL look the same wherever you find it (currently TSO, CMS, CICS, VSPC), but they still have a long way to go to do it. The bureaux, on the other hand, have diverged rapidly from VS APL, and have developed shoals of quad functions to handle everything from error trapping to file access. In the short term this is clearly to their advantage, but it does clutter up the language with a lot of very un-APL instructions. I know IBM's way of pushing everything out into auxiliary processors is harder to work with, but it does preserve the purity of the original concept. It would, however, be very convenient to have facilities like)LOAD and)COPY as part of the language, rather than messing about with an input stack. Automatic 'house-keeping' on the symbol table would be very welcome too, or at the very least some way of clearing it without the rigmarole of ')CLEAR,)SYMBOLS,)COPY,)WSID,)SAVE'. I know of at least two occasions when ')CLEAR,)SYMBOLS,)WSID,)SAVE' has lost a day's work! I've no idea who will win this one, and I don't really care, as long as all the necessary facilities are made available one way or the other. On the whole it seems likely that VS APL will have to follow APL*PLUS, this being the only way IBM will pinch back significant amounts of business.

I know this is supposed to be a look into the future, but it seems to me that a brief review of the various IBM environments might be appropriate here. VS APL is currently a fully supported 'program product' under CICS (a transaction processor designed for online enquiry/update), VSPC (a time-sharing supervisor running within MVS – IBM's main batch operating system), and VM/CMS. This last provides every user with his own 'virtual' computer, and a cut-down operating system with which to drive it.

VS APL can also be found (and frequently is!) under TSO, which is effectively a full-scale, time-shared operating system. Of the four, CICS is very much a way of getting a few people hooked ('Not more than six concurrent users' say IBM, and I believe them), and TSO is thought to be a bit long in the tooth, and probably on the way out. That leaves VM/CMS and VSPC, which (as environments for APL) are superficially similar, but there are some quite important differences in detail.

First the similarities – both support execution of host commands; use of local files (APL format and EBCDIC); full-screen; input stack; and external VSAM files. So far, so good, but life is rarely as easy as that! The two most obvious differences are that CMS provides an easy route to 'off-line' APL (VSPC does not), while VSPC supports user-to-user shared variables (CMS thinks everybody is 1001!). Another noticeable contrast is in the maximum workspace available: it is a generous 16 megabytes under CMS, and 4 megabytes with VSPC.

The less obvious differences only become apparent when you want to do something slightly subtle, such as imitating APL*PLUS's component files. CMS handles direct access, variable length, APL-format files – which is just the tool you need; VSPC does not. Under CMS you have a complete 'virtual system' to go at, with card-readers, card-punches, and printers; getting a deck of cards 'into' VSPC is a work of art! As for routeing output to fast printers (or remote work-stations), it *can* be done under VSPC, but you won't find it easy. The other major contrast is in the hosts themselves, with CMS providing a powerful 'EXEC' language, and VSPC a somewhat feeble-minded equivalent. Even as simple an operation as clearing the screen becomes a labour of love in IBM's flagship of 'personal computing'.

Finally, how do the two compare on the one yardstick that really matters: response time? I can do no better than to quote from 'Making the inhouse decision', again from *APL in Practice*:

'VM/370 is a superior interactive time-sharing system with terminal response time in the two second range . . . . MVS is a superior system for batch processing and an adequate system for an ancillary, low volume time-sharing workload (if five-second response time is acceptable to the user community)'.

Enough of IBM! There is one more feature of the APL*PLUS system which holds fascinating possibilities – ACE or 'Automatic Control of Execution'. This is effectively a way of running APL jobs automatically in a kind of quasi-batch mode; it makes obvious sense for regular production runs, and for heavy one-offs like workspace documentation. However, it also raises the possibility of concurrent processing, where several active workspaces co-operate (using shared variables) to achieve a result. It is this avenue that I now want to explore, because it seems to me to offer all sorts of possibilities in the developing field of process control.

In Chapter 13 I dwelt at some length on the rather artificial distinction which has arisen between 'Data Processing' and 'Office Automation', and I suggested that APL is well suited to both fields. A similar distinction divides systems which basically process information from systems which control and monitor machines: APL cannot yet bridge the gap but there are clear signs that it may. The essential problem is that big mainframes are deaf, dumb, and blind to anything that doesn't obey some precise and complex protocol. They also suffer from widely variable response times, and a 5 s delay in closing a valve could trigger a major disaster.

This demand for instant, reliable response is met by the simple expedient of dedicating a mini-computer to control each cluster of machines; the IBM system/7 is such a computer, and has been the subject of a very interesting implementation of APL (Alphonseca *et al.*, 1977). Using shared variables, this APL can issue requests such as

```
AI MOD 5,POINT 14,INTV 200, NVAL 10
```

to read 10 consecutive values (at 200 ms intervals) from point 14/module 5. The result is an APL vector (length 10) of values in millivolts. Suppose an electric kettle was plugged in to a microswitch (activated by 500 mV) at point 12; to make tea, we would place

```
AO MOD 5,POINT 12
```

into the control variable, and 500 into the data variable. This may seem an odd use of APL, but the fact is that many process control systems must handle matrices (e.g. 200 readings from 10 sensors), often of binary values. APL is clearly an excellent tool for this particular job, but more important is the possibility of unifying, say, a production planning system with the actual machines being planned. A possible configuration would be

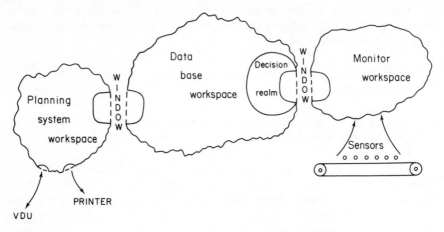

In this case, the traffic is one-way only: the sensors attached to the plant return information to an APL workspace, which aggregates it in some way, and logs it periodically into a database (probably another APL workspace in practice). This information can be accessed when needed by a production planner, who can use it to make up-to-the-minute judgments about possible changes of schedule.

The next stage is obviously for him to feed such changes of plan back into the database, ready to be picked up by the control workspace, which will then take appropriate action. Clearly, further workspaces could take care of such tasks as ordering materials, working out the wages, analysing absentee statistics, ensuring a sensible maintenance schedule, and so on. The beauty of such a unified approach is that the possibilities are virtually endless, and with APL shared variables, and distributed decision making we can exploit them to the full.

That is my view of one possible future; it is obviously conditioned by my personal experience, which has been of VS APL used 'in the raw' for a wide variety of decision-support systems in a large and complex manufacturing company. I have placed very little stress on the development of APL packages, because I have never yet come across an application which could not be more easily satisfied with a purpose-built system. Building-bricks and system utilities, of course; but somehow the next level up never *quite* seems to work as well. Perhaps it's just that my company does things in strange and unusual ways (e.g. a 13 month year), or perhaps the world is not as simple as the package-writers would have us believe? We shall soon see who is right!

Finally, I would like to close this look ahead with another quotation from Professor Ackoff. In his view, the classical Operational Research paradigm 'Predict and Prepare' contains an inbuilt contradiction, since by preparing for the future we invalidate our own prediction! He suggests a new paradigm:

'... design a desirable future, then invent ways of bringing it about'.

APL is just a better way of inventing desirable futures.

Epilogue

My experience in computing has been of interactive BASIC (at university), several years of batch PL/1, a bit of FORTRAN, Z-80 assembler, and APL. I approached APL with a fair degree of suspicion - surely computing couldn't be *that* easy? - but (always happy to try something new) I used it to have a crack at a production planning system which had become rather bogged down in PL/1. In about two months I had progressed from an unwieldy tray full of cards, an algorithm that didn't work, and a reluctant user to an enthusiastically received system which produced useful results at remarkably little cost.

Since that time I have learned a lot about APL, but the basic conviction that it is simply a 'better way' remains as strong as ever. I know there are jobs it can't tackle - payroll for 100 000 people, huge LP problems, making tea - but these are ruled out by limitations in the environment, not by any deficiency in the notation. APL is still years ahead of its time - one day it will do all these things, and with a clarity and simplicity that will astonish the computing world.

The systems thinking of today has been brainwashed by the need to process data one element at a time; this has led to programming languages like BASIC and PL/1, and to an impressive range of techniques generally known as 'structured design'. All these tools embody one (fatally flawed) assumption about the world - that it is hierarchical. They assume that data is held in files; files are composed of records; records are composed of fields. This is *not* true. Data is composed of patterns which may overlap, interleave, and interlock. It is only our limited view that has forced it into such an artificial and unrealistic structure - of course we can dream up a design method which will produce 'perfect' programs in such an over-simplified world!

No such design method exists for APL, because in APL you can see *all* the data *all* the time - usually it's quite obvious what you want to do to it, and usually your requirements can be expressed as a couple of APL symbols! One final example: a company prints 9999 special-offer slips, and sends out all those which don't get chewed by the addressing machine, pocketed by employees, etc. It records the numbers of those it actually sends, and logs the numbers of the replies received. The object is to send the manager a report

Offer no.	Result
1	Never sent, no reply
2	Sent, no reply
etc.	

for the four possibilities. (If there are any replies to unsent offers, some luckless employee is doubtless due for the high jump!) For one solution see 'Principles of

Program Design' (Jackson, 1975); the point is that if you are forced into processing one item at a time from the two separate lists (SENT and RECEIVED) then this really becomes rather a difficult problem. You must correctly synchronize the way you read the files, and you must also cope sensibly with the possibility of running off the end of either, or both. Why do we insist on making life so difficult for ourselves?

Traditional programming methods produce difficult solutions to trivial problems, and cannot hope to tackle anything subtle. APL treats trivial problems (like the one above) to trivial solutions, and gives us hope that it will not make the difficult ones impossible. In writing this book, my overwhelming feeling has been one of ignorance; of just how little we know about these new tools called computers. We are in much the same position as the engineers of the eighteenth century – building steam engines without any idea of the laws and science of thermodynamics. Their machines worked (after a fashion); occasionally they blew up and killed people; their development was painfully slow – but they worked, so people kept on building them. Eventually, one or two very clever people began to understand *why* they worked, and suddenly we had steam locomotives which could pull a train from London to Aberdeen in eight hours.

The day is still a long way off when a computer will reliably deduce that 'Time flies like an arrow' is semantically rather different from 'Fruit flies like a banana', but that day will come, and the development and spread of APL has brought it significantly closer to hand. I hope this book may have made some small contribution to the development and spread of APL.

Appendix: Recommended reading

This appendix is split into three sections: general background; books about APL; and references to the specialist literature. It largely reflects my own reading habits and preferences, and obviously is not totally representative.

Background

Under 'background' I would include most of the regular computing magazines, and two works of literature: *The Machine Stops* by E. M. Forster and *Future Shock* by Alvin Toffler. Another powerful contribution to the debate is *The Mighty Micro* by Dr Chris Evans. Finally, everyone who writes dialogues should hear Arthur Dent's altercation with the Nutri-Matic Drinks Synthesizer from the BBC radio programme 'The Hitch Hiker's Guide to the Galaxy' (Series 2, Episode 2) (also published in book form as *The Restaurant at the End of the Universe* by Douglas Adams). It stands as an awful warning to us all!

APL Books

Next the APL books, and one stands head and shoulders above the rest. *'APL – An Interactive Approach'* by Gilman and Rose gets better every time I read it. They have achieved the remarkable feat of producing a book which can be understood by the novice, yet read in bed by the expert with undiminished pleasure. I hope they never change it! Another old chestnut is Paul Berry's APL\360 Primer – I have never seen a better introduction to what APL is and does. It *reads* so well, for one thing, and it's a far pleasanter way of learning the language than ploughing through one of those dreadful PI texts.

On the theme of learning APL, there is *'APL: The Language and Its Usage'* by Polivka and Pakin, and *Structured Programming in APL* by Geller and Freedman. The latter is quite a good APL tutor, but only actually mentions structured programming twice – on the title page and in the epilogue! Both of these seem to me to be books to get from the library to read once; you want Gilman and Rose on your desk as a permanent fixture!

At the next level up, most of the literature is of a rather mathematical/technical nature; however, I would recommend *APL in Practice* for general reading. As might be expected from the proceedings of an STSC conference it is somewhat bureau-oriented, which means that you have to wade through a host of 'Isn't our package wonderful – please buy it' papers. Nevertheless, there is plenty of good stuff there, and you may want a 'bureau' perspective to balance my 'in-house' view! Of course

176

there is more to writing a good APL system than just knowing APL, and James Martin's *Design of Man–Computer Dialogues* should be included in any APL training program.

List of References

Cited in chapter

Ackoff, R. L. (1978). The future of operational   2, 13, 14
    research is past. *J. Oper. Res. Soc.* **30**, 93–104.
Alphonseca, M., Tavern, M. L., and Casajuana, R. (1977).   14
    An APL interpreter and system for a small computer,
    IBM Systems J. **16**, 1, 31–38.
Berry, P. *et al.* APL\360 Primer, IBM GH20-0689-1
Evans, C. (1979). *The Mighty Micro*, Gollancz, London.
Geller, D. P. and Freedman, D. P. (1976). *Structured
    Programming in APL*, Winthrop Publishers, Cambridge,
    Mass.
Gilman, L. and Rose, A. J. (1976). *APL – An Interactive
    Approach*, Wiley New York.
Jackson, M. (1975). *Principles of Program Design,* Academic   Epilogue
    Press, London.
Hammer, M. and Zisman, M. D. (1980). Design and   13
    implementation of office information systems. Infotech
    State of the Art Reports.
Martin, J. (1974). *Design of Man–Computer Dialogues*,
    Prentice-Hall, Englewood Cliffs, N.J.
Polivka and Pakin, (1975). *APL: The Language and Its
    Usage*, Prentice-Hall, Englewood Cliffs, N.J.
Rose, A. J. and Schick, B. A. (Eds.) (1980). *APL in Practice*,   14
    Wiley, New York.
Tobin, N. R. (1980). The changing role of OR, *J. Oper. Res.*   6
    Soc. **31**, 279–288.
Waldbaum, G. (1978). Tuning Computer Users' Programs,   3
    IBM Res. J. 2409–31920.
Werder, A. (1979). *Crab-APL*, Issue 6, December, p. 15.   8

Index

179